T0278322

The
Green Gardening
Handbook

The Green Gardening Handbook

Grow, Eat and Enjoy

NANCY BIRTWHISTLE

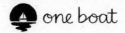

First published 2023 by One Boat
an imprint of Pan Macmillan
The Smithson, 6 Briset Street, London EC1M 5NR
EU representative: Macmillan Publishers Ireland Ltd, 1st Floor,
The Liffey Trust Centre, 117–126 Sheriff Street Upper,
Dublin 1, D01 YC43
Associated companies throughout the world
www.panmacmillan.com

ISBN 978-1-0350-0371-6

5 7 9 8 6 4

A CIP catalogue record for this book is available from the British Library.

Illustrations by Ruth Craddock

Typeset in Adobe Caslon Pro by Palimpsest Book Production Ltd, Falkirk, Stirlingshire
Printed and bound by CPI Group (UK) Ltd, Croydon, CR0 4YY

Visit www.panmacmillan.com to read more about all our books
and to buy them. You will also find features, author interviews and
news of any author events, and you can sign up for e-newsletters
so that you're always first to hear about our new releases.

To my grandparents, my first teachers,
who would have been proud of this book.

Contents

AUTUMN

WINTER

LET'S GROW!

When I say this is a gardening book, or more specifically a growing at home book, I have to confess to you before we start that I have never been to horticultural college, joined a gardening class, entered a show, or in fact ever documented my garden and growing knowledge apart from posts online to my social media friends and a short chapter in my last book, *Green Living Made Easy*. I have, however, been growing fruit and vegetables for well over forty years, in gardens of differing shapes and sizes, and have even more distant memories of my first involvement in the garden with my grandfather and that would be over sixty years ago now – crikey! I have read lots and lots about growing – after all, there are encyclopaedias and books of many volumes on the subject. I have gathered as much information as my head can process from both reading and doing, resulting in, I believe, a fairly sound understanding of the growing, harvesting and preserving of the food that I like, that then keeps me stocked up for the best part of the year.

No matter what size of growing space you may already have or want to create, whether you have a thundering great allotment plot, an area of the garden you want to develop as a food-growing space or a fabulous sunny spot on a balcony – whether you are a homeowner or renting – you can get something from this book.

This book covers growing in small spaces and helpful hints and tips for beginners as well as several new little environmentally friendly nuggets I have recently acquired to benefit the more experienced gardeners who are wanting to adopt a 'greener' approach to growing their own food.

I have fun in the garden – I like to try new things, not always sticking to well-documented rules and advice – and suggest you have the confidence to do the same. Most of all, as you flick through the pages of this book I want you to feel empowered and excited about having a go yourself.

I know very few Latin names for plants so you will have to forgive me if – when I write about growing and harvesting cauliflowers, for instance – I fail to refer to them as *Brassica oleracea* var. *botrytis,* and that – when I get so excited about a bumper crop of summer strawberries – I ignore the fact that one strawberry is a *fragum* whereas a bowlful would be *fragaria*! The horticultural Latin used for naming plants is a cocktail of Latin, Ancient Greek and a plethora of other languages from Russian to Mandarin, so there you go: not knowing the Latin is not going to hinder our success in the garden, though if there is a particular variety of seed with a peculiar sounding name that has worked well for me, I'll give that a mention. For those who want to get going but they don't know where to start, it all feels too complicated, and they don't have the necessary skills, tools or confidence, let me assure you that nature does most of the work and, once you've harvested your first radish, lettuce or strawberry, you'll want to try to grow more and more!

By collating the knowledge that I have gleaned over the years and by putting it into some semblance of order, I have done my very best to write sensibly about how I grow my fruit, herbs and vegetables and a few (mostly edible) flowers. I discuss composting and how I plan my gardening year, what to do with gluts of fruit and veg, and have included a number of my favourite recipes plus tips on how to keep your harvest for longer. I also discuss how to keep plants in containers, soil and greenhouses abundant and free from disease without having to resort to harmful chemical treatments, fertilisers, pesticides or insecticides.

I hold up my hands and admit that in the past I had been guilty of considering organic gardening to be a chore and thought that it could not possibly be that effective and instead was relying on weed killers, pesticides, sprays and chemical fertilisers to, so I thought, produce the best crops.

Several years ago, I began my green journey and this way of thinking has now permeated every part of my life, from the way I clean my house to the way I resist single-use items, recycle and upcycle where possible, am mindful about the use of valuable energy and utilities and also how I have been able to apply this way of thinking to my garden. I became more informed through researching and reading while considering the plight of our natural world and am now converted to methods that, once the penny drops, actually make utter and complete sense, and are logical and sensible. Once we learn how to work with Mother Nature and understand how the seasons work, how plants behave and how we can harness the wonder of it all, the reliance on any destructive chemical, synthetic or harmful methods for home growing are utterly superfluous.

The mental health benefits of gardening are also very encouraging. These include a reduction in symptoms of depression and anxiety, an increase in attentional capacity and self-esteem, reduced stress and improved mood. This is certainly true for me whenever I am outdoors. There is nothing finer for my own wellbeing than a good day's gardening. The big wide world with its troubles and strife can be set aside for a time. Instead, my attention is turned to the buzz of insects up close, a new green shoot on my camelia (which I thought had maybe given up), seeing the daily changes on fast-growing cucumber plants and the nostalgic scent when I prick out the side shoots of tomatoes. My hands and clothes are grubby, my hair tousled and dishevelled, yet I feel relaxed and happy. This is me – this is where I am and where I want to be. Following a good gardening session, I am feeling physically (not mentally) tired, the fresh air outdoors has given my cheeks a rosy glow, I am looking forward to a hearty plate of home-grown food then an early night and I sleep like a baby!

There are no failures in gardening. Maybe there are one or two disappointments but let me promise you there is fun, enjoyment and nothing less than an absolute thrill when you lift a leaf to find your first hidden shiny tiny red tomato that can be pulled warm straight from the vine and enjoyed there on the spot. This is unique and something the shops and supermarkets with their plastic-wrapped, perfectly shaped, sized and brightly coloured wares are unable to do.

I have included a number of seasonal recipes with storing and preserving tips. So much fresh produce is now available all the year round in the supermarket, which means our food seasons are less well understood. This results in demand for food products being such that to satisfy our appetite fresh food is flown in from all over the world. I am fortunate to have enough garden space to enable me to become less and less reliant on supermarkets and shops for my fresh food, but no matter how big your space there is always plenty to grow and do. When I need to buy fresh food, I increasingly try to only buy seasonal produce that has been grown locally. It has taken some years to get to this point, however, and I am mindful that as a young mum with young children, cost was always the main driver when shopping for food, and was probably one of the reasons I started growing my own. We all unwittingly pick up fresh produce in a supermarket without even considering that the price is high because it is out of season, but by taking our first steps into following the gardening calendar we begin to appreciate more about what is in season and when things are at their best. Once you start growing yourself or spotting a 'top notch' seasonal offer in the shops it is no surprise then that the household budget will begin to stretch further.

Last winter, I visited a restaurant and cast my eyes over the menu to see asparagus pop out at me. In the UK, asparagus has a short season of about six to eight weeks from mid spring to early summer – it tastes delicious and I have grown it myself. Trouble is, I had so few plants that once I had harvested the beautiful tender spears, I had eaten them raw before I'd made it back to the kitchen! Due to the time of year, the asparagus on this menu may have been flown in from far afield in polystyrene and cling-film packs, having been harvested some time back and subjected to an array of 'in-transit' temperatures and conditions resulting in an inevitable lack of taste, colour, texture and freshness compared to the same vegetable at its seasonal best. The same applies to the pack equivalents on display in the supermarket.

If you don't like a particular fruit or veg, it may be that you have only eaten it out of season when it is not at its most tasty and tender. We have all had a powdery apple or two, or a hard pear, not to mention the stringy stick of celery that will bend and have to be unthreaded rather than snapped before being crunched and munched!

I have not always appreciated the seasonality of food. I remember a holiday in France where I had decided I would entertain some friends and make blackcurrant jellies for a dessert with a set white chocolate cream on the top. They were to be served in cocktail glasses and would look decadent yet interesting, with a fresh berry or three on the top (like flower arranging, I always arrange decorations and garnishes in odd numbers). It was early autumn and I took myself off to the supermarket to search for fresh blackcurrants. No joy, not a blackcurrant in sight so I asked where I could find them. 'It's not the season,' I was told. When I looked further – just about every fresh vegetable in the supermarket was home grown and marked 'Origin de France'.

Each year I am getting better. I buy less out-of-season and imported food, relying instead on my delicious though limited selection of home-grown produce plus a top-up from the local fruit and veg shop or supermarket, and once in there my aim is to choose mostly seasonal and therefore less expensive foods.

Children also love to get involved in gardening. It helps develop their understanding of the natural world, learning about what plants need in order to thrive – that they too need food to be fit and strong, that insects are not enemies and most of the time they are friends. Having some input into the production of their daily food may result in children (and adults!) being less picky when it comes to mealtimes. Food grown outside and under the ground actually gets a bit grubby! I've been racking my brain to think about when it was that food started to be washed before going on sale. Back in the day, potatoes were sold with a layer of dirt, as were carrots, beetroot and other root vegetables. Have you noticed that even though they may be washed and packed neatly in plastic wrap or bags the instructions on the pack still advise to wash before use? Makes me wonder about the hidden secrets in the water they use to wash them!

A basic understanding of where our food comes from is fundamental to the health of our planet and ourselves. We are part of nature and I believe once you've grown something of your own from scratch, tasted it in its unspoilt, un-stored, sprayed, treated or, at worst, processed state – your respect for fresh home-grown food will hold a special place for you. I remember – probably over twenty years ago now, well before I had grandchildren – a neighbour's eleven-year-old child used to pop in to play with our then-new puppy. She used to help me in the garden from time to time and I can remember so clearly her squeals one day when she helped me to unearth potatoes. 'This is SO cool, she said – potatoes come out of the ground!' This innocent comment made me realise and appreciate the worth of helping my grandad as a child.

Children take it in and soak up all kinds of information when they work alongside you, whether in the kitchen or out in the garden. I try to encourage my own grandchildren to get involved and the fantastic thing about gardening is that they can spill and make a mess – it doesn't matter. Even the smallest hands can fill a pot or tray, plant seeds and water them in – they love it! Small children adore puddling around in water and there is nothing finer on a summer's day than giving a small child a little watering can to water their seeds and plants – it keeps them busy and they learn as they go. They then wonder with delight as they see their garden grow; they learn to take responsibility and understand that, just like a pet, plants are living things and have to be looked after . . . priceless!

Growing food is not only fun, it is informative too, and I firmly believe that once we understand the seasons, that the supply of food is finite, and that food waste is unnecessary and costly, we can live a healthier lifestyle that in turn will ensure our planet stays healthy too.

I have organised this book into seasons so that, with a better knowledge and understanding, you may want to resist imported foods in favour of those in season that have been grown as close to home as we can manage. As well as doing our bit for the planet, I feel certain you will actually begin to notice that locally grown, or even better home-grown, food at its seasonal best is varied and exciting, has much more flavour and as a bonus we know that it has not been stored for a long time before being transferred to the supermarket shelves and as a result will cost less too.

Where to Start?

My response to the beginner or first-time gardener is to start wherever and whenever you like. There is always something to do in the garden, yard, balcony or other outdoor space. A seed that can be sown, a plant to be re-potted, an area of land to plan, weed and improve, and usually there is something to harvest. Whatever your growing space, this book shows you how to grow, harvest and preserve food while appreciating the need to respect the natural world and understand that it too, like me, has its own need for food, wellbeing and habitat in order to stay healthy. Planet Earth and nature are not separate to us – we are part of them, not the other way around.

Growing is cyclical. I have tried not to be too prescriptive about start and finish times in this book and, in fact, I have been pleasantly surprised by successes that have been achieved when planting and experimenting during periods traditionally considered to be too early, too late or simply not the right time. I offer hints and tips on what to look out for and when and how to be prepared, be on guard so that little irritating issues don't become big gardening problems.

This book is divided into easy-to-use seasonal sections or chapters – twelve in all, three for each season – with specific guidance for 'newbie' gardeners who are starting out on this very rewarding pastime.

In the UK, spring includes the months of March, April and May whereas a reader picking this book up in New Zealand will be enjoying springtime from September to November. For this reason, I refer to seasons rather than months – early spring for me is March, mid spring April and late spring is May, and so on. Dialogue I have had with followers worldwide would suggest that some plants may be a little different from country to country, but the majority are generic and some climates suit certain plants better than others. Nowadays, we can take advantage of modern inventions and can speed things up, and improve conditions by growing under glass, in an electric propagator, a cold frame or even an upcycled plastic box. We are able to enjoy certain fruits and veggies that in the past may have been considered 'exotic'.

I am often asked why I bother growing my own food and my answer always is that it is fun, tastes better and I know it has not been treated or sprayed with a cocktail of chemical additives to keep it in show condition. My home-grown fruit and veggies may not be the most beautiful – they're probably slightly misshapen and wonky, and many a carrot or parsnip will have two legs. The main point is that I have known every radish, tomato, cabbage, apple and beetroot from the beginning, I have helped it to grow and mature, tried to keep it free from danger and disease and – one thing is for sure – if you grow your own food you will not waste a morsel. My fruit and veggies, whether wonky or not, will be eaten. They teach and enable me each year to understand more and more about the natural world.

Learning as You Go

I now know my tomatoes split maybe because I didn't water them consistently, my parsnips grow multiple roots because I may have planted them too close together in poorly prepared soil, and my onions bolt and go to seed maybe due to a cold snap which shocked them into thinking they need to reproduce quickly before they die off. I will make some notes and then next year I can build on this when I plant again.

On the plus side, my apricot tree produced an abundance of perfect fruits after I tackled the canker (see pages 248–9), and I made lots of jam and dried fruits to last over a year. A single packet containing just 50 broad bean seeds yielded an amazing 3kg (nearly 7lb) thanks to my rich home-produced compost (pages 25–35), so that's broad beans for the winter, and my football-sized perfect curly savoy cabbages shielded from the cabbage white butterfly simply with a layer of netting – duly captured on photos – are the talk of the town!

Gardening is always a challenge and, increasingly, with extreme weather patterns results are less predictable and so very often no two growing seasons are the same. There are good years and not-so-good years. A bumper year for peas one year may be followed by a feeble show the following year – but for me that is the excitement and intrigue of engaging with nature and learning year after year more and more about something I will never know enough about.

Take It Easy

Gardening and growing, with all the moving, bending, stretching and walking – also keeps me fit. It gets me outside and keeps me grounded (in more ways than one). The natural world is far from simple yet it's quiet calm seems to put problems and worries into perspective. Mother Nature cannot be rushed into doing things before she is ready, and I love that real and gradual slow progression as the garden moves from season to season. There is no pressure to get this done or that – I can work at my own pace, nothing will spoil, even the split tomatoes and wonky veg mentioned above will be fully used, all is not lost. Plants may overgrow and weeds may pop up here and there, but that is just fine, this is just nature doing her thing. A good weeding session, similar to a good cleaning session, is so rewarding and satisfying once done.

I don't need to put on any airs and graces in the garden, there's no one to please – just myself. There are no 'What shall I wear?' issues or, 'Are my hair and makeup okay?' I am what I am and every other living plant or insect that I come into contact with in the garden has come just as they are too. None of us is pretending to be something we're not or worried about what anyone might say or think.

I realise now that I absorbed much more than I realised in those years I spent in my grandad's garden as a child. There are certain jobs and smells in the garden that immediately take me back in time and I have recollections as though they were just yesterday. The unearthing of potatoes, the pinching out of tomato side shoots and the sweet rosemary-type smell of flowering currant bushes in spring. These memories are so nostalgic and one of the reasons I now spend time with my own grandchildren baking, crafting, gardening, sewing, etc. They will absorb some of it without realising and then be able to recall it later when needed, I hope.

Making Room

Each and every one of us has a different growing space. Maybe you are a proud allotment holder or you have a veggie plot in the garden already, or you may be excited about turning a disused spot in a courtyard, balcony or even a sunny window-sill into a place to start to grow food in pots and containers of all kinds. I now have a large growing space for fruit and vegetables, plus a greenhouse and, even though I have a large area in which to work, I have also grown fruit and veggies in a small container garden (about the size of a small balcony) with astounding success. The message really is whatever your space – please have a go!

Growing in pots and containers in a limited space is incredibly rewarding and can yield fantastic crops. A selection of barren pots seeded in early spring will be unrecognisable and completely out of sight by midsummer, the whole area having been taken over by lush, green leaves, colourful flowers and finally bearing an abundance of edible gorgeousness. Mother Nature wants you to succeed, plants actually want to grow – those seeds are there patiently ready and waiting.

Salads, beans, courgettes, tomatoes, carrots, onions, potatoes and beetroot will grow in containers and even the most unusual vessels. I grew the best crop of radishes (French Breakfast) ever in a dented deep loose-bottomed non-stick cake tin – the loose bottom meant I didn't need to make drainage holes and the non-stick prevented any rust. Each one was perfectly shaped, without a blemish – absolute beauties. This tin method for radishes is now a keeper for me, as the bulbs and leaves so often get nibbled when sown direct into the ground. Growing in this way I can eat the whole radish – root, leaves and all. I have grown 'cut and come again' salad leaves, basil, parsley and sage in the bottom half of milk bottles covered in a layer of sacking for decoration – these did need drainage holes. Again, very practical as they sit nicely on my outside kitchen windowsill and I simply reach out of the window and cut what I need – and I can water them from inside too!

Let's Get Out There!

For many, the gardening year starts as the weather warms up, the days get longer and tiny plants and seed packets appear in the supermarkets and shopping centres – usually late winter and early spring but before this time it is well worth having a good think and actually to plan your crops. By doing this you will avoid an inappropriate impulse buy or, just like food shopping, buying too much because you are carried away by the colourful display or 'buy one get one free' type offers. My hope is that wherever you are in your gardening year you will be able to find out what jobs can be done, what can be harvested, the problems you may well encounter and, last but by no means least, the foods that will be in season in your garden along with a number of my favourite recipes and a selection of methods of preserving.

So, whether you are a complete novice and want to begin your growing in a few small pots, on a sunny balcony or in a yard, but don't really know where to start, or you're someone who has recently started and wants to try new things, or an accomplished gardener who is striving for a 'greener', more sustainable plot, or someone who has access to fresh home-grown produce and would like a few tips on preserving or storing for longer – I think you will enjoy this book.

After covering some garden generalities I will now move onto the gardening year. It is my plan that wherever you are in the year when you pick up this book, you can turn to the appropriate time in the season, have a look for a few garden jobs, know what can be sown or harvested and enjoy a seasonal recipe or two.

WARDROBE

Before delving into the practicalities of growing your own food – I would first like to talk a bit about the gardening wardrobe. Daft as it may seem – I cannot enjoy a day, or even just a few hours, in the garden if I am not wearing the right clothing and footwear. If I start swanning around in my best jeans and jumper or tee shirt – I can be sure I will pull the jumper on a thorn, get a grass stain on the tee shirt and mud on my best jeans.

I have what is always referred to as my 'gardening gear' that is kept in the bottom of my wardrobe. Two pairs of old jeans, two tee shirts, a black and white jumper (that is badly pulled and snagged) and an orange fleece that is peppered with tiny bonfire burn-holes. Once I get outside, I don't know where the day will take me, but I am always so comfortable – the clothes are roomy, I can kneel and crawl around on the ground, I can get mucky without having to worry about stains. If I get too hot, I can toss the fleece onto the ground, if I get even hotter, off comes the black and white jumper that I often hang on a tree, leaving me in my very off-white cotton tee shirt which is perfect for working in.

When it comes to gardening gloves there are many on the market. I tend to work with bare hands, especially during the summer when the ground is dry. However, for pruning and working among certain weeds and nettles a sturdy pair of gloves is advisable. A good pair of garden gloves is a great gift idea for the gardener.

I have black leather working boots for the garden. I've had them years and they are very comfortable – I can kneel and move around freely, which is not so easy in wellies. I gave these boots a complete makeover recently, making weatherproof and gorgeous once more – see page 55 to find out how.

||||||||||||||||||||||||||||||||||||||||||||||||||||||||||||||||||||||||||||||||||||||||||||||||||||||||||||||

UPCYCLE TIP: If you wear rubber gloves in the garden, as I do for certain wet jobs such as cleaning plant pots and the greenhouse in early spring, you will inevitably get a split or tear in one glove. Rather than tossing the gloves into the bin to end their days in landfill, keep the good undamaged glove and pair it up with another or turn it inside out if you find yourself with two left-handed gloves. Cut the damaged glove into strips. Starting at the cuff end, the rimmed cuff of the glove becomes a great device for keeping sleeves rolled up. The rest of the glove can then be cut into rubber bands, even the fingers. I use these to keep bunches of plant labels together, wrap around half-used packets of seeds and wrap around garden canes to keep them all in one place.

||||||||||||||||||||||||||||||||||||||||||||||||||||||||||||||||||||||||||||||||||||||||||||||||||||||||||||||

BASIC EQUIPMENT

Over the years I have accumulated a whole range of tools but my favourites of all are my oldest and dearest, gifted to me by my grandmother when I moved into my first house that had a garden, back in 1976. She bought me a Ladies' set of tools,

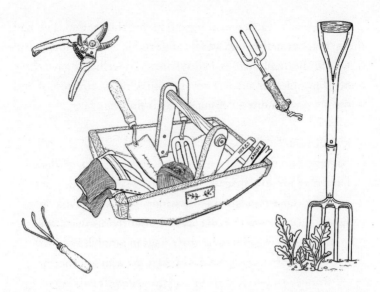

perfect for smaller people, juniors and budding gardeners. My gift consisted of a small spade, a rake, a hoe and a garden fork. Over the years, the fork has needed a new handle but other than that each piece of equipment is still going strong. If you are starting out, it is a good idea to put an item of gardening equipment on your birthday or Christmas list. Santa is very good when it comes to practical gifts!

Here's a list of what I consider to be the most useful pieces and for those starting out with a container garden – a handy trowel is all that is really required.

Tools

spade
garden fork
hoe

rake

the best secateurs you can afford

edging shears (if there is a grassy area)

hand trowel

airtight and waterproof tin or box for seeds

pencil

plant labels

bamboo canes or sticks

biodegradable jute twine

watering can with a fine rose attachment

spray bottles for homemade sprays (or upcycle a used milk
    bottle to make a fabulous watering can which is ideal for
    pots and very young seedlings – see page 273)

Pots and Planters

For those just starting out, it is not necessary to have to splash
out on fancy seed trays and pots because there are a number
of everyday items that can be upcycled to make excellent seed
trays, plant labels and planters and I will come onto that later
(see pages 246-7). If you are planning to buy new items there
are lots of sustainable choices meaning you don't have to invest
in plastic items.

Buckets, made of plastic have been around a long time
and I had stopped thinking outside of the box when it came
to buckets. When my old faithful plastic garden bucket split,
I spotted a range of bright coloured plastic ones in the
hardware shop but then, tucked away in a corner, were
rubber and metal alternatives. Seeing them immediately
took me back in time. I remember those – brilliant! My
replacement bucket doesn't have to be made from plastic

and metal or rubber can be more hard-wearing and easier to repair.

That's it! That's all the kit you need to get started. Taking care of your equipment will ensure it enjoys a long life: after use, always clean tools down with a simple wipe in dry weather but in wet or damp conditions make sure the tools are thoroughly washed and dried before storing inside. When your tools are put away for the winter, wiping them over with an oily rag will protect them from rust. Secateurs particularly need to be cared for if they are to live a long life: wipe them down after use to remove dirt, then rub the blades with an oily rag, and to keep them sharp try cutting them across a used piece of folded sandpaper several times. This will keep them in tip-top condition. Always store them in the closed position, too.

CLEAN KIT, HAPPY GARDEN

Avoid being the creator of your own problems. Bear in mind that when using garden secateurs, loppers and even scissors – or in fact any similar tool you take from plant to plant – they can also spread disease.

Let me tell you about my blackcurrant bushes since the fruit just happens to be my favourite soft fruit berry. Some years ago I had six beautiful bushes in their own bed. Every year they fruited well and every winter I gave them an annual prune. One particular year one of the six bushes failed to thrive – it was covered in buds in the spring but then the leaves appeared looking rather feeble. The plant didn't fruit as did the other bushes and, compared to its neighbours, looked quite forlorn. At the end of the year I cut it back as part of my annual prune and then went on to cut the other five back too. The following year all six bushes suffered the same plight.

After doing some reading and investigating, what I had was 'blackcurrant reversion' – the advice was to dig up the plant and burn it. The disease is spread by mites which are not very mobile but I am certain in my case I helped them along by moving from bush to bush with my secateurs and inadvertently spreading the disease. I was devastated because my whole blackcurrant collection had to be destroyed and burnt.

As a result, I am now very careful when pruning or cutting back, taking extra care to sterilise my pruning shears or secateurs whenever I move from bush to bush or tree to tree or where I suspect something may be looking troubled, diseased or dying. To keep secateurs and clippers clean – rather than resorting to harmful chlorine bleach or buying proprietary products – a thorough wipe with a cloth dipped in surgical spirit or hand sanitiser will do the job. Spread it around the tool, leave it on for 20–30 seconds then wipe off with a cloth to sterilise and kill any hidden bugs and disease.

PLANNING YOUR GARDEN

The garden or growing space requires a little planning so I invite you now to have a think with me about how best to use your space.

The way I do it – which to some may seem a bit dated in our modern technological world – is to have my diary handy. It's a large A4 'page a day' one and is amazingly useful for reference to know when I did things. I jot down sowing and planting dates, harvest dates. I also make notes about the smallest of things such as which date in mid spring I spot the first Swift – usually around 5th May. I have two huge copper beech trees and each year their resplendent fire glow of leaves can be enjoyed from around the 26th April!

My diary of memoirs during the 'not so active' garden months becomes a great space for making drawings and plans for the garden. Having everything in one place ensures I can always put my hands on my notes rather than jotting here and there and then losing the information.

I will go out with my diary, a pencil and tape measure and draw a simple diagram of the plot – this approach makes organising the future growing space much more real. When I planned my container garden, I scribbled the various pots and planters onto paper too.

When you sit down to consider your next growing year, take time to ponder, stare at the ceiling and ask yourself the following questions:

- Is the growing to be done in pots and containers?
- Is there a greenhouse and/or cold frame?
- What about a compost area or bin – where is the best place for it?
- Do you want to get a head start and maybe think about a propagator?
- Do you want to attract more wildlife, more pollinators into the garden – is there space for a wild garden, an insect house and bird feeders?
- Do you want a place to relax – to sit and enjoy the space you have created? Do you want to enjoy this space in sunshine, in the morning, the evening or most of the day?

My container garden

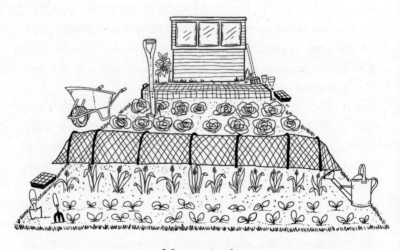

My veggie plot

I've included some diagrams that I used when planning parts of my own garden to help you think about what might work, so that no matter what size of growing space you have, you can maximise and make the most of it.

Your plan is not set in stone, of course, and when it comes to planting you may want to change things around a bit, but it is so much easier to have a template to work from. A dwelling house would not be built without a plan and the same applies to the home for our glorious fruit and veg!

WATERING AND FEEDING

When growing in pots, it is necessary to have a regular watering regime. When plants and veggies are in the ground a shower of rain will easily be absorbed, yet with plants in pots, it is still necessary to water the containers. As foliage grows and leaves get bigger and bigger throughout spring and summer, the welcome drink of water from a shower of rain simply runs off the leaves onto the balcony, patio or yard rather than be absorbed by the compost in the pot.

When planning your garden consider a water barrel, trough or butt. Or more than one if you have the space. I am always excited to hear the water butt filling up during a summer shower of rain. Surface rainwater is perfect for garden and houseplants and much better for them than precious tap water.

In addition, add a feed to your watering plan to help your crops do the very best they can from what is essentially a limited supply of food in their pot.

Tomatoes are particularly hungry, so a weekly feed added to the daily drinking water (I always feed them on a Friday – no idea why, but I then don't forget) will make a huge difference. A liquid organic tomato fertiliser will be perfect not only for your tomatoes but for other veggies and hanging baskets too. I start to feed tomatoes once I see flowers on the plants and continue until harvest time. Other veggies in pots and containers and my flowering hanging baskets get a half-strength feed once a week. I've included a few recipes on plant feed you can make at home, see pages 180 and 285–7.

CURIOUS ABOUT COMPOST?

Compost is our garden's food and the key ingredient that will ensure our soil's health. It is nourishment, a weed suppressor and moisture retainer and is produced following a natural process that turns organic material (things that were once living) into rich soil-like material. The organic material is miraculously broken down by worms, insects, fungi and bacteria plus wondrous chemical reactions, and what went in as solid waste comes out as a sweet-smelling dark, crumbly rich natural loam, plant food and fertiliser for use in the garden.

Making your own compost, or should I say, allowing Mother Nature to make your compost for you, is a magical experience. We all recognise the brightly coloured plastic sacks for sale in the supermarkets and garden centres and those enthusiastic gardeners just starting out may need to buy their initial supplies. If you don't have the space to make your own compost, or your own compost isn't ready and you are eager to get started on your gardening journey, buy a 'peat free' variety as composts containing peat are depleting essential peatlands. Peat and peatlands are hugely important for plants, the wildlife that depend on them and, ultimately, us humans too. Peatlands store vast amounts of carbon which must be kept in the ground to avoid contributing further to climate change.

TIP: The large colourful plastic bags that contain compost can be reused. I tend to turn them inside out so that the gaudy colours are on the inside, make a few air holes here are there, then use them as compost bags for fallen leaves in the autumn. Once packed full, give them a good watering, fold in the tops, stand a heavy stone or brick on the top and store in a corner of the garden, leaving the leaves to decompose and go on to make a gorgeous top dressing for plants and veggies in the garden. Alternatively, I cut the bags into pieces and use them to line hanging baskets and wall-mounted hayracks (which I then plant with geraniums), black side of the plastic facing outwards.

Create Compost

I would recommend that composting becomes a part of your starter kit as you get involved in the garden. Just as growing food is becoming more and more popular – whatever space is available – so is composting. There are so many kits available to suit every taste and space including wormeries, simple counter-top composters, black bins of varying sizes and then pallet-style constructions for those with more space. I take huge satisfaction each time I add something to my compost bin, knowing that it is one less item going into landfill.

When I was a child, the compost heap in my grandad's garden was simply an 'out of the way' dump where every piece of garden waste was thrown. I remember he used to turn it from time to time with a special garden fork that had just two long prongs – probably a hay fork. He used to tuck the fresh waste underneath, bringing the dark, well-rotted compost to the surface. I was too young to know how good his compost was, though I fondly remember his amazing crops.

The bins available to buy nowadays are much more sophisticated and the large often re-cycled plastic boxes can be loaded from the top and, if you do it right, the resulting beautiful compost is harvested from the base. Compost bins are available in various sizes to suit your space but can be quite pricey and it's much cheaper to make your own if you or someone in the family is handy with wood and screws. A bottomless compost bin can be constructed very cheaply if you are able to get hold of old pallets of wood that can be refashioned to make a wooden slatted box. Similarly, a large plastic box with a lid can become a home compost bin but remember to include lots of ventilation air holes. Compost needs good air circulation for decomposition to take place, ensuring that the heat inside destroys the weeds and seeds and so that all shapes and sign of any original plant is transformed and becomes a dark brown crumbly material.

There are benefits of an enclosed space versus a heap like my grandad used to have, yet each have pros and cons. Firstly, a bin looks better rather than a scruffy heap with un-rotted banana skins, potato peelings and egg shells on the top. Secondly, a bin is less likely to get smelly in the summer months because the layering (see opposite) is easier to do therefore the composting process gets working quicker. Once a compost bin is full it can be covered and then left to do its work. If like me you make composting a habit and want to keep recycling your own kitchen and garden waste you may go on to make a start on a second bin, then a third – you'll be rocking and rolling! The danger with a heap is that it is never full and instead keeps being added to and then becomes so huge that it is a massive job to access the good stuff right at the base. A heap on the other hand is cheap. Simply find a place in the garden to start to pile your material for compost. A heap can be easily watered from time to time, and turning the outside to the inside using a garden fork thereby ensuring even decomposition is easy to do.

So, how does it work and how long does it take? For a compost bin to start working it needs air, heat and moisture and, of course, some material to start working on. A sunny spot in the garden, rather than a dark shady corner, will provide more heat that will quickly kick-start your compost maker. There is lots written about composting but rather than confuse you (or me) with lots of different recommendations from other gardeners and growers, this is my tried and tested method.

If you have done any reading about composting you may hear gardeners refer to 'brown' and 'green' layers being added to the bin to ensure best performance but I find this sometimes difficult to grasp, and until I started composting seriously and with purpose I didn't even know that 'layering' was a thing. My early composting years were simple – I slung everything onto a heap, in no particular order – just as veggie waste occurred. When my bin was full I covered it with a piece of carpet and left it to do its work. Some months later anticipating the much-awaited rich sweet smelling crumbly black loam, I would lift off the carpet top to see this beautiful natural creation – so satisfying. However, as I delved deeper into this rich dark goodness, I would also then come across a layer of stinky non-rotted grey and mouldy-looking grass clippings or thick non-decomposed sprout stalks not to mention the odd rogue plastic plant label and (can you believe) my long-lost hand trowel! Why had this happened, why did it smell, why had some things not decomposed and what was I doing wrong? I now understand that for the compost bin to work well and at its best it needs a balance of green material and brown material, so start to think about the items for your compost bin as two basic ingredients.

The green seems at first easy to understand – green stems and leaves, green kitchen vegetable scraps, grass cuttings and prunings. So far so good. I also add coffee grounds and tea leaves to my compost bin so are they brown or green? And what about manure from the likes of my chickens or from horses, sheep and hamsters – brown or green? Although they look brown, with further research they are actually green so to avoid further confusion I developed my own easy method. I have decided that to make it easier to grasp and to get your layers right – I refer to the layers as WET for green and DRY for brown. In simple terms the wet ingredients get to work quicker and the dry slow things down – therefore an even mix will produce a balanced bin!

I will start with the wet items that we all produce from the kitchen: apple cores, fruit peelings, tea leaves, coffee grounds, vegetable peelings, banana skins and spent cut flowers. Then, the wet items from the garden, including lawn cuttings (without any weed killer), small prunings and dead-headed roses and blooms, hedge clippings and weeds. Large stalks will break down but to help them along, chop them into 15cm (6 inch)

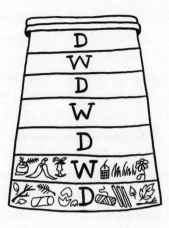

lengths first using a spade – I used to sling the whole lot in – stalk, roots, any remaining leaves, etc. – no wonder it was a huge job for the worms! All of these items are rich in nitrogen or protein and are the ones that will tend to heat the compost pile up because they help the microorganisms to grow and multiply quickly. Other nitrogen-rich items that fall into the 'wet' department are fresh manure from rabbits, chickens, horses, sheep, etc.

WET
apple cores
fruit peelings
vegetable peelings
tea leaves
coffee grounds
banana skins
faded cut flowers
faded garden flowers
hedge clippings

weeds

grass cuttings

hedge trimmings

sprout stalks, bean stems, sweetcorn cores, etc., cut up into
15cm (6-9 inch) lengths

The dry ingredients are the carbon-rich materials which are
slower and more resistant to decay. These will be incorpo-
rated among the wet ingredients so that everything
decomposes at a steady rate and will provide a good bulk
to your compost and ensure a constant supply of food for
the microorganisms busy doing their work. Dry ingredients
include dead leaves, straw, cardboard and paper (not shiny
backed paper), pine needles, small dead twigs and stalks

and I include egg shells here too, though some would argue they are wet not dry and as they have probably been tossed into your kitchen waste anyway, they don't really matter. I also add the contents of my vacuum cleaner bag which is simply household dust and detritus. Be sure not to include any plastic or paper clips that the vacuum might have sucked up, though.

DRY
newspaper
packing paper (not shiny or glitter)
old beeswax wraps
vacuum cleaner contents
dead leaves
straw
used compost
pine needles
small twigs
egg shells
cardboard
biodegradable string and twine
dried flower arrangements
used luffa scourers
coir matting or brushes
sawdust
natural cotton ribbons, strings and strands of wool (I use
    these for gift wrap, no nylon or manmade items)

Things that shouldn't be added to the pile are cooked food waste containing any meat, fats or dairy as this can attract vermin. Diseased or infected plants should not be added to the compost and need to be burnt or disposed of (see The Mini Bonfire on page 232).

When it comes to metal ties, plastic clips and plastic plant labels, try to remove them before they get to the compost pile otherwise they will come out looking just as they did when they went in. I am moving over to biodegradable jute twine and wooden plant labels for use in the garden, so that any oddments that fail to be removed before composting will decompose along with everything else.

To simplify things even further, try to visualise the cross section of your compost bin as a huge multi-layered double- or even triple-decker salad sandwich. I like mine packed with crisp moist green salad (the wet ingredients) and sandwiched with layers of dry wholemeal bread (the dry ingredients). Various gardeners suggest exact ratios of green to brown or 'wet to dry' but I tend to work on a rough 50:50. Whatever your preferred ratio, your bacteria and fungi will be happy. In the summer months when the compost material may be dry, or after adding a layer of 'dry', I often water my compost pile to help things along and create some action. Once the box or bin is full to the brim I top it off with a piece of old carpet to keep the heat and moisture in. I then start a second bin or pile. You will never have more compost than you need, so the more bins you have room for the better. Once your bin is full and covered, leave nature to do its work.

You will know whether your compost pile is performing well simply by lifting the carpet and laying your hand over it. If your pile is busy you will feel the warmth on your hand – you may also see the tiny red wiggly worms dancing around and partying to their heart's content. These are the best compost worms – they prefer compost to plain soil and I was amazed to see that they are available to buy online! I have never had the need to buy worms – they just arrive and move in themselves and once the compost is ready for use there will not be a worm in sight – they will have found a better home with well-stocked cupboards. I found that once I embraced a greener approach to living – in the garden and in relation to my food – I was ever more appreciative and amazed by the wonder of nature, especially the creepy crawlies, and because of this will continue to do my very best to cherish and preserve it wherever and whenever I can.

If, like me, you find composting fun, invest a few pounds in a compost thermometer: it will keep you entertained for hours and is a great talking point with enthusiastic gardening friends. I actually did a video to prove to 'Him Indoors' that my compost

bin was steaming! The temperature outside was 20°C (68°F) and the thermometer read from the compost pile was a staggering 50°C (122°F)! How fantastic! A compost thermometer is also a great gift idea for the keen gardener. The hotter your bin, especially when sitting in a sunny spot as mentioned above, the faster that huge salad club sandwich will decompose and be transformed from a number of layers to a rich, black sweet-smelling loam. It is a wondrous and fantastic process – the heat being created from the activity of the microbes in your bin, raising the temperature of the composting material.

FAQs

CAN I PUT WEEDS IN MY COMPOST?

Yes! Don't be afraid – I used to think they shouldn't be added, but a properly managed compost bin will easily reach 50 to 60°C (140°F) which breaks down all organic matter including weed seeds.

HOW LONG DOES IT TAKE TO MAKE COMPOST?

The answer to this is anything between six months to two years, though I have found that if the layers are right, your compost will be ready sooner rather than later. If you examine your pile and there seems to be a sludgy area that smells awful then you probably have a wet layer that is too thick. This can often happen if the pile has a thick layer of grass clippings without any dry material. The best thing to do here is to take a garden fork and give it a turn around. Take out the layer of stinky sludge and add it back in thinner layers among the pile, breaking it up and spreading it around with some dry paper, dry leaves or garden soil or spent compost from trays of pricked out seedlings, end of season containers and hanging baskets.

You will know because the pile will smell sweet – similar to that gorgeous steamy earthy smell that comes from the ground after a summer thunderstorm. The loam will be dark, moist and crumbly. There will probably be fewer insects and worms weaving around because they have eaten everything they need and will have moved onto the compost pile next door.

Down With Digging!

Your ready-to-use compost is now rich in food and nutrients for your fruit, flowers and veggies. Use it to fill planters and top-dress rose bushes and fruit trees. Lay a good thick layer over your veggie plot in the autumn and early winter and the worms will do the work of taking it below the surface – no need for you to embark on a full-body workout digging it in.

Gone for me are the days of 'double digging', the back-breaking job of creating deep trenches each autumn (hurting worms in the process), laying compost into those trenches then back-filling with the top of the next trench. I used to do this religiously each autumn and it took me weeks because, as it was such hard work, I used to limit myself to one or maybe two rows a day. My grandad used to do this and he grew great veggies and – having done some reading around it – there is no wonder he favoured this approach. It was a new method adopted in the 1960s which was then considered the 'organic' way forward, in a move to replace the ever-growing market for (and over-use of) synthetic chemical fertilisers.

Thankfully, this labour-intensive, back-breaking method has now been replaced by a much gentler approach. I now improve my soil and prepare my garden applying an organic 'no dig' method – simply topping my weed-free soil with a good layer of compost. The soil underneath remains undisturbed, precious carbon remains locked into the ground, the worms and other insects are free from injury and can therefore be capable of doing their own fantastic job of incorporating and spreading goodness into the earth. The soil remains moist and healthy, the balance of nutrients is maintained and I rarely need a long soak in the bath to recover from a day in the garden. The only digging I do now involves the gentle preparation for sowing seed or transplanting a seedling, the exciting unearthing of a potato, carefully easing out a parsnip or simply taking a hand trowel to uproot an onion.

Having a good compost to offer your garden will result in strong, healthy, disease-free plants and crops that retain moisture too. No need to buy costly and often harmful synthetic chemical fertilisers or treatments – the more natural the better!

Keen to get cracking? Let's GROW!

SPRING

EARLY SPRING

I can feel and smell the excitement of spring in the air as can the whole of nature. The birdsong ramps up and what were hard, tiny buds on bushes and trees are now beginning to colour, soften and fill out. Smiling and giggling young spring flowers show off their bright clean hues as they sway from side to side in the freshening breeze and longer hours of sunshine.

I try to refrain from cutting my spring flowers – I prefer to enjoy them for longer as I walk around the garden. The exception, always, are the poor souls who have put so much time and effort into growing tall, delivering the most beautiful bloom only to then be flattened by a gust of wind. I walk around and gather these broken individuals, then pop them into a vase so I don't need to see them end their days as rain splattered and battered fallen heroes lying flat on the ground.

Once the temperature reaches around 10°C (50°F), the first 'forager' honeybees can be seen busily hunting and gathering following their long sleep. Ladybirds will make an appearance too – spring has sprung!

Lots of sowing can be carried out in early spring, though don't be too strict on yourself – when you examine seed packets there is usually a two- or three-month window for sowing. If you are eager and want to start early with certain crops, go ahead. I find it is the only way to learn and understand growing conditions for certain crops. If a few seeds fail to germinate there is still time for a second sowing in mid to late spring if the early sowings didn't go to plan due to a severe frost or cold snap. Early spring is time, too, to pop seeds into a mini propagator if you have one. Sow tomatoes, cucumbers, peppers and aubergines – and even nature's own pan scourer and bath puff, the Luffa gourd (but only if you fancy a challenge!).

Just a note about propagators. If, like me, you're eager to get started, a small electric propagator (a great gift idea), will give your seeds a head start and germination will take place in just a few days after sowing. Bear in mind, however, that if you have the little plants ready to be pricked out and moved into large pots too early, the ambient temperature even in the greenhouse may be too cold for them. I once did just this – I was so impatient to get going with my new piece of kit that I planted my tomato and cucumber seeds in late winter only to find that after a couple of weeks I had a huge number of healthy seedlings ready to be moved into their own pots. These tender young plants need a temperature of 12–15°C (54–60°F) to be able to grow on and flourish, yet the weather outside was around 7°C (45°F) and probably only about 10 or 11°C (50–52°F) in the greenhouse. They had to stay in the propagator for longer than I would have liked, otherwise my efforts would have all been in vain. One thing is for sure – you can't rush nature.

Limited Harvest

Early spring is probably the leanest time in my veggie plot. I'm determined not to buy food out of season from the shops and supermarkets, so it's important that I make the most of what I have. There are a number of leeks, parsnips and remnants of kale and spinach still doing their very best and, along with my over-wintered apples and frozen berries and beans, this keeps me going.

Seasonal Spring Gifts

For Mother's Day (in the UK), Easter and other spring present-giving occasions, rather than be drawn into the supermarket displays of last-minute gifts (such as bunches and bouquets of imported fresh flowers, planters made to look bigger and more colourful with the addition of excess packaging and bright cellophane), gift your home-made and home-grown creation. I promise anyone will cherish a hand-made gift over a purchase that has cost much more than its value.

Spring flowering bulbs – prepared and planted in the autumn (see page 219) – make great Christmas, Mother's Day and Easter gifts. Get the kids to paint plant pots or, an even cheaper option, upcycle a plastic pot or even the base of a 3- or 4-pint milk bottle.

Kicking Off the Year's Planting

Just as sowing in the greenhouse may begin to take place, for the container gardener and those starting out, similar planting can take place too. If you have been saving single-use plastic trays, pots, milk bottle bases, or have already a number of useful containers, they can be planted with seeds. The seed packet may advise 'sow under glass' during early spring and if, like me, you want to get going this can still be achieved.

I have a huge plastic clear storage box with a clip-on lid and this became a perfect mini greenhouse once I turned it upside down. I stood my various mini trays of seeds on the lid (so they were lifted from the cold ground), gave them a good watering and then covered the whole lot with the upturned box. This was hugely successful. I had created my own mini cold frame! Once the sun shone on this brilliant piece of kit my seeds were off to a great start.

By the end of the season, I find there will be welcome warm days, but the nights are still cold. These conditions are perfect and will not harm the hardier crops such as cabbages, cauliflowers, sprouts, leeks, parsnips and broad beans but heat and sun-loving veggies such as tomatoes, cucumbers, peppers, basil and aubergines will feel the cold.

As mentioned, I have often given in to temptation and sown too early but now every year I sit on my hands and wait a few weeks before sowing these more tender yet worthy crops. Even if you don't have a propagator, when ready to sow these seeds can be started on a sunny windowsill indoors and once the weather warms up and the plants are growing you will be one step ahead.

Encourage Bushy Growth

As your early seedlings get going and produce their first and second sets of leaves, nip out the second pairs of leaves. This encourages the plant to branch out along the stem and creates a fuller plant. Sweet peas sown in late winter should be ready to be nipped out in early spring.

Cold Shock

Growing under glass in a greenhouse, cold frame or a plastic box provides a warm, humid environment which tender seedlings love. Imagine that you are laid out on your sun lounger, soaking up the rays, feeling the sun warming your whole body then someone comes over with a hose pipe and pours it all over you. The reaction is shock – you jump from your bed and curse the person that thought this was a fun idea! The same goes for seedlings – there they are basking in the warmth and sunshine then you decide they need an icy shower. The result – shock. And in the worse cases this can damage their young tender leaves.

Whether in the greenhouse or inside the plastic box I keep my full watering can of rainwater under cover too, so that when I water my tender plants, the temperature of the water will feel just right – not icy cold from the tap or rainwater barrel. Obviously when the spring and summer arrive this is not an issue, but in early spring the temperature in the greenhouse and container frame can be many degrees higher than the water temperature in the tap.

PLANTING

I routinely check my seed packets for this season's planting that can be done straight into the ground when conditions allow.

A handy fireside job is to sort through packets of seeds to check sowing and harvesting times and plan accordingly. Among my packets of purchased seeds, there will be envelopes containing seeds I have saved myself, duly labelled and sealed. I am interested in trying this more and more (and saving money too). I haven't bought sweet pea or runner bean seeds for years, or parsnips either.

‖‖

TIP: When it comes to choosing seeds – for flowers, fruit or veggies – you might be overwhelmed by the selection on offer for just one single item. Take onions, for example: there are so many seeds to choose from, plus small bulbs (sets), and of those there are so very many varieties. One packet may contain lots of seeds, whereas another more expensive F1 hybrid (I call them Formula One) may have a tiny number in comparison. The Formula Ones are apparently top quality, promising vigour, uniformity and good yield, and this is reflected in the price! I tend to choose varieties that have been around a long time, have been tried and tested and are good value for money. I always read the packet to discover a bit of history about the variety and while I have splashed out and bought the expensive seeds from time to time, I can't honestly remember there

being a marked difference in the resulting produce. To
be honest, I get much more pleasure when growing
from seeds I have saved myself. The seeds you save
from the F1s will not be the same as their parents
because you can't control what they are pollinated with.

Save seeds – any seeds. I place wet seeds on kitchen paper and
leave them until they're dry and free-flowing, then store them
in small sealed paper envelopes, labelled and ready to try the
following spring. My favourite variety of tomato is Marmande.
They're large, beefy and a perfect all-rounder so I save their
seeds and root side shoots too (see page 141).

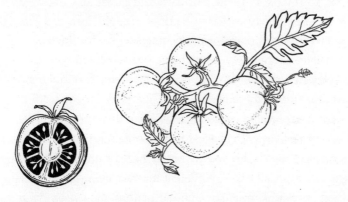

When a crop has done very well in my garden, I like to
experiment by leaving one or two plants alone, not harvesting
their fruits so that their flowers hopefully go on to produce
seeds. I remember feeling disappointed when my row of tender
leafed rocket produced coarse stems and began to flower. I
considered pulling them all up to start again until, to my amaze-
ment, they became a great restaurant to a whole range of insects

and pollinators. Needless to say I left the show of bright yellow rocket flowers to those that needed them the most.

Don't be afraid to have a go. My friend once gifted me a small plant about 10cm (4 inches) tall in a 7.5cm (3 inch) pot – a baby orange grown simply from a pip. I still have it. A horse chestnut tree started in a small pot from a conker can become a family heirloom!

I sort my packets into sowing seasons then, along with my plot planner, scribble my rough growing ideas so that I will know roughly when and where to sow. I secure each sowing season's seeds with bands (my bands are made from reused rubber gloves – see page 16). I now feel organised.

For me the conditions are just right when the earth doesn't cling to my boots yet is still dark and moist and the weather isn't too cold. My earliest plantings straight into the ground are broad beans, parsnips and potatoes.

Broad Beans

I love fresh broad beans and they are also a fantastic crop for freezing (see page 151). One packet of around 50 seeds plus a 'good year' will keep me in broad beans until the following season. One pack will be sufficient for the sowing of a 3.5-metre (12-foot) double row (sowing instructions are always given on the reverse of the packet) which are usually to plant the large seeds 5cm (2 inches) deep and 23cm (9 inches) apart in both directions in a double row. I often find I have a few leftover seeds, so I pop them into 7.5cm (3 inch) pots, water them and set aside. The beans that are sure to germinate in the pots can be used to backfill any that fail to germinate in the ground. If you like broad beans, they will prove to be a good starter crop.

They don't ask for much, are easy to grow and they are a brilliant high protein, highly nutritious food.

Parsnips

Growing parsnips is easy. They're not always perfectly shaped but they're good and tasty nonetheless. Parsnips can be sown straight into the ground over the coming weeks but do choose a still day: the seeds resemble small slivers of tissue paper and a sudden gust of wind will send the seeds flying into the air resulting in your neighbour enjoying a crop of parsnips rather than you! I get down on all-fours when sowing parsnips – I like to be close to the soil so that these tiny seeds can be transferred from the palm of my hand to the shallow row with minimal chance of displacement.

I discovered some years back that old parsnip seeds don't germinate well. In fact, a packet of seeds from the previous year didn't germinate at all! Using last year's seed works really well for many crops but not parsnips, so for them I always use fresh seeds. However, I have overcome the need and expense of buying new seed each year.

If, like me, you want to grow parsnips every year don't harvest them all – leave two or three in the ground to grow on purely for seed. The first year's foliage will die down in winter, to re-emerge the following spring as the weather warms up. These little beauties with the fresh green growth, now a year old, will become my next year's seeds – it takes two years in all for a parsnip to produce seed. When these new leaves from last year's crop reach 5–7.5cm (2–3 inches) in height I carefully dig them up and transplant to a place where they can grow on. Remember there will be a long parsnip root to remove so be sure to dig down then carefully lift without snapping. Choose a sunny spot absolutely anywhere in the garden – not necessarily the veggie bed though they do attract insects away from your favourite crops.

This is a fun thing to do – the parsnip plant will grow about 1.8–2.5 metres (6–8 feet) tall, produce huge flowers and then by late summer will dry off and provide seeds. I will cover this later when we discuss collecting seeds (see page 162). Your enthusiastic gardening friends will probably have no idea what it is you are growing as you show them around your garden at the height of summer. I have found, even if not grown for seeds, the tall parsnip plants are huge insect playgrounds. I spent one sunny afternoon marvelling at the activity – aphids, ants, ladybirds, wasps, butterflies and bees. They were all on the dancefloor making their own music while busying up and down the long stems and flowers, and I applauded them for finding parsnip flowers more interesting than my cabbages and sprouts.

Leeks

Any garden or growing space should find a place for leeks. Easy to grow and extremely hardy, they are a versatile veg that doesn't take up much room. Early spring is the time for sowing the small black seeds. I used to believe I was getting ahead by sowing them even earlier in trays under glass: they started off looking like thin blades of grass then I pricked them out into cells in trays, then transplanted them to their final growing area in late spring. Apart from the time it took to do all of this I often found my leeks would bolt and go to seed and had no idea why. One year, I was well behind with my sowing and instead of sowing leeks under glass I put them straight into the ground in early spring: I simply sprinkled them into a shallow row, labelled them and that was that. Several weeks later I had a perfect sturdy row of what resembled very small spring onions. Fast forward several months and not a single one bolted or formed a seed pod. This has been my preferred method ever since.

Raspberries

Of all the soft fruits, raspberries are a favourite, mainly because they are so easy to grow, and, unlike strawberries, will crop from the same plant for many years. I grow two types – summer- and autumn-fruiting varieties. This guarantees fresh berries from early summer right through until late autumn (some years even stretching to early winter, depending on weather conditions).

Now is the time to plant summer fruiting raspberry canes – so called because they are not bush-like in appearance. If

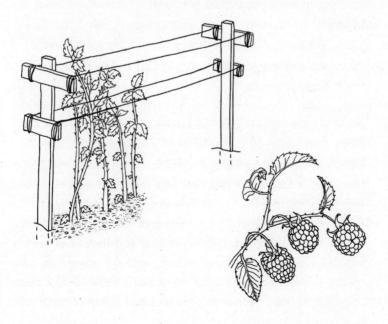

you buy them from the garden centre at this time of the year they will resemble one or two sticks stuck in a pot!

Raspberries need supports because, when they get going, they will be tall and leafy and need to be secured to wires. If you decide to grow raspberries, the frame structure should be created first before the plants go into the ground.

For those with less space – or for whom the erection of a frame, wires and the like seems like a lot of work – invest in an autumn-fruiting variety. Although later to fruit (mid to late summer), they need no supports so there's no need to tie them up and you will have berries right up until the first frosts. I choose the variety 'Autumn Bliss' – it never fails.

Strawberries

Plant any overwintered small plants about a foot apart and as the weather warms up they'll soon get going. Or leave them in pots/planters – they'll be happy almost anywhere sunny.

Potatoes

The seed potatoes that were set aside to 'chit' in mid to late winter (see page 265), by the end of this season will be displaying tight dark purple shoots about 2.5cm (1 inch) long and now is the time to plant them in the ground. Even though Easter is a movable feast – my grandad used to plant on Good Friday (weather permitting) – I tend to choose any dry day when the sun is shining between now and mid spring.

TIP: To help you make straight rows for seed sowing and planting out, take two pointed sticks about 46cm (18 inches) long (mine was originally a broom handle and the top of the handle that contained a hole became a threading and securing area for one end of the rope) and fasten to each stick a long length of thin rope. This is now a great home-made tool for marking rows. Simply put one stick into the ground then take the other stick and the rope to the other end of your planting area to determine a perfectly straight row. Any surplus rope can be wound around the stick to make the length tight.

Neat rows of veggies at the height of their growing season look almost too good to eat but, as well as looking fantastic, a neat row has a purpose as it is much easier to identify weeds popping up (they may look very similar) either side of the tidy row and remove them early so that they do not starve your baby seedlings of precious nutrients and moisture.

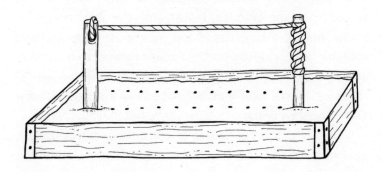

I have two methods for potato planting. I use Method 1 if I didn't get around to prepping the bed the previous autumn (but Method 2 is much easier). Both methods yield brilliant, delicious crops.

METHOD 1

After marking a row for the potatoes, create a trench. I have an old draw hoe which is very handy for creating the trench in one go. The flat-surfaced tool is pulled through the earth, creating a flat-based trench with soil piled up either side. If you don't have a draw hoe then a standard hoe or the corner of a small spade will carve out a suitable planting trench though it may be more 'V' shaped rather than flat bottomed but that is fine, the potatoes don't mind. Pop your chitted spuds 30cm (12 inches) apart along this trench, then use the piles of soil either side to cover.

I don't want to disturb any of those fresh shoots as I pile the soil over them, so I first surround them with a good handful of soft compost and – if the grass has been cut and there are fresh clippings (not treated with fertiliser, weed killer or the like) – I sprinkle them over each potato too. This keeps them moist, protects the little shoots and, according to my grandad, helps protect against attacks of potato fungus. I have added the fresh grass clippings to a compost layer at every planting for as long as I can remember and have never suffered potato fungus. It could be one of those 'old wives' tales' but it has become a nostalgic habit that is hard to break.

Carefully pull the soil over to cover the potatoes using a garden rake then create a mound of earth above the row about 30cm (12 inch) deep. This 'earthing up' of the row will protect the growing potatoes from frost, keep them moist and will encourage heavier crops. Earthing up also keeps the potatoes well buried so that they will not turn green through exposure to light. Green potatoes should not be eaten. If a growing potato is exposed to light it will start to go green which indicates the development of solanine and may upset digestion and cause illness. Eating lots of green potatoes could cause extreme reactions.

Potatoes will grow in most soils and even if you don't have a well-prepared bed, simply dig a hole with a trowel and pop a chitted seed potato in there. If you have simply made a hole and popped in your chitted potato then it is still important to pile over a mound at the outset or continue to add extra soil or compost as the leaves appear.

METHOD 2
The year I wrote this book I carried out an experiment – I love a trial! I planted two varieties of potatoes and for both varieties I used two different methods. One method was to dig a trench as mentioned above and the second was to pile earth into rows – looking really as though the potatoes were already planted. I started this the previous autumn, adding compost and leaf mould then simply leaving it all winter. By early spring one or two weeds had taken hold which I could easily pull out; I then tidied up and redefined the mounds with a rake before using a dibber (a pointed tool – a cut off handle from an old spade is perfect) to make a deep hole, pop in the potato and cover. That was my potato planting done and it was so much easier.

So far, my plants have never suffered from potato blight which can result in a whole crop being lost to disease. However,

I only grow 'earlies' which are ready to harvest in midsummer which, from what I understand, is before blight arrives.

I am sure there are potato growing experts who suggest doing much more to encourage a successful crop, but I now just wait for the green leaf shoots to appear, I keep the bed weed-free and well-watered if there is a dry spell, then wait for what is – for me – one of the best days of the gardening year: the first potato root in summer.

SEASONAL TIP FOR BIRDS

Your planters full of spring flowering bulbs will be resplendent, your veggie growing pots and containers may be sown and you want them to remain undisturbed. I want to attract birds into the garden but prefer that they don't take a liking to my favourite pots and the fresh compost and young green shoots that are a huge attraction. Birds at this time of the year will take great delight at pecking around if they think there could be seeds or something fresh and new to forage.

I keep small animals and birds (in my case, pigeons) off my freshly sown beds, young seedlings and strawberries either by constructing netted frames on my large plot or creating covers for my container garden from simple everyday items. On the large plot, chicken wire can be stapled onto wooden frames or, even better, fine reusable netting, and there are biodegradable options that can be purchased, which will keep birds off in the spring (and the cabbage white butterfly in summer too). A perfect row of cabbages can be eaten alive by an army of newly hatched caterpillars in late summer, but by netting them off from the time they are planted they will be kept safe and secure. For those with smaller gardens and container gardens, I have found a number of improvisations that work well.

Lay a small metal rack (I think mine was originally from a grill pan) over the top of 2 or 3 small newly sown pots – it's a fantastic bird-proofer.

Thread plastic bottle tops onto strings and suspend them across growing areas. As the wind blows, the strings sway from side to side and – unless pigeons are good limbo dancers – I doubt they are willing to risk being hit from behind by a brightly coloured milk bottle cap.

TIP: Save orange and yellow netting bags from packs of lemons and oranges to cover the top of single pots. The plastic netting stretches, so can be pulled across even the largest of pots then secured around the neck with a plastic band (or use the cuff of an upcycled rubber glove – see page 16).

WATERPROOF OLD LEATHER BOOTS

My comfy leather boots – part of my garden wardrobe (see page 16) – had developed creases after years of bending which meant they eventually gave way to moisture and after walking around in the long grass I realised my socks were getting wet. Was it time to discard my old keepsakes? With my upcycling hat on I decided to give them a make-over and weather seal them, which worked brilliantly.

YOU WILL NEED
damp cloth
clean soft brush
spent candle
hairdryer
dry cloth

My cream cleaner
100g (3½oz) bicarbonate of soda
35ml (1¼fl oz) vegetable glycerine
10ml (2 tsp) eco-friendly washing-up liquid
jar with a lid

To make the cream cleaner, simply weigh the ingredients straight into the jar, stir with a spoon, seal and store. This paste will also clean up any white garden furniture brilliantly and has many uses around the home too (more on that in my book *Green Living Made Easy)* but let us not digress.

||||||||||||||||||||||||||||||||||||||||||||||||||||||||||||||||||||||||||||||||||||||||||||||||||||||||

NOTE: do not use lemon washing-up liquid because the paste will separate and become hard. The lemon reacts with the bicarbonate of soda.

||||||||||||||||||||||||||||||||||||||||||||||||||||||||||||||||||||||||||||||||||||||||||||||||||||||||

Remove the boot laces then clean the boots thoroughly using the cream cleaner. Use a damp cloth dipped in the creamy paste to remove dirt, grease and any residual shoe polish (though that had long since disappeared in my case), then leave them to dry out.

Once dry, brush off the powdery residue. Your boots will be clean but rather dull looking. Take the spent candle and rub wax into every nook and cranny. When I finished my boots they looked as though they were covered in a layer of frost.

Take the hairdryer and blow hot air over the boots and within seconds the wax will melt and be absorbed by the leather. Use the dry cloth to gently massage the wax onto the boots an even coating and hey presto: weatherproof boots!

You've no idea how happy this made me. I treated my boots to a new pair of laces and was so pleased. No silicone sprays or waterproofing products and, best of all, no need for new boots.

EXTENDING THE SHELF LIFE OF YOUR PRODUCE

Carrots add flavour and colour to meals and have so many uses, though I have not yet managed to grow them in sufficient quantities to keep me going right through the winter. When I buy them, I go for unwashed carrots as I find they keep well in a cool garage for several weeks whereas washed supermarket carrots sold in plastic bags last just a matter of days, going soggy, mouldy and sprouting if not looked after.

I carried out an experiment and couldn't believe the results. Has anyone else experienced this? 'Him Indoors' was going out and asked me if I wanted anything from the shops. 'Yes – a bag of carrots,' I said. He came back with two bags – 'Why two bags?' I said, 'They were cheap' was his reply. I went into the pantry only to find another unopened bag of carrots! I had so many carrots . . . around 3kg (nearly 7lb) if I recall.

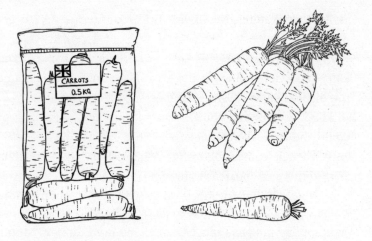

Food waste is a huge problem I am always ranting about, and I knew that if I left these carrots in their plastic bags, within a few days the whole lot would be soggy and would end up being tossed into my compost bin and – in other households without recycle facilities or compost bin – the whole lot, plastic bag and all, would have to be slung into the general refuse bin to end up in landfill.

After following the steps below, I didn't lose or waste a single carrot. I made soups, casseroles, carrots with every meal and some very tasty veggie snacks. The weeks rolled on – by week three I had used most of the carrots and by week four was down to my last few. At week five I had one carrot left so decided to see just how long this beauty would keep. At this time of the year, root veggies – even those from the supermarket – will begin to sprout. You know the bags of potatoes that once looked good to eat have now wrinkled, grown long white shoots and wound themselves around each other? Carrots and onions too will soften and start to sprout as Mother Nature gives them the springtime nudge to get moving.

My carrot however, chilling in the fridge was still firm, no hairy roots developing or tiny leaves. My final carrot became the inspiration for 'Carrot Saturday'.

Many veggies and fruits will stay fresh for longer if kept damp and cool. Wondering about what happens to the nutrients when it comes to storing veggies, I did some reading around this and apparently vitamin C rapidly diminishes after harvesting. (A huge advantage on the vitamin C front therefore for those of us who grow our own!) Other nutrients such as antioxidants and carotenoids, however, actually increase as the stored veggies mature and sweeten.

What about the taste, you may ask? My carrot experiment went on for six months – can you believe it? At the end of this time, I decided to peel and chop the carrot even though by this time I had got quite attached to her. The carrot was still moist, had no blemishes once peeled, was firm with a perfect colour, and had the same taste and texture as any other carrot.

Since that fateful day I have challenged many fresh fruits and veggies and given them the secret to a longer more youthful life, trying it successfully on washed carrots, celery, parsnips, swede, spinach, cucumber, courgettes, rhubarb and peppers – the list goes on and on. I may take to wrapping myself in damp towels and sleeping in the fridge! There is a table on how long you can store fruits and veggies on page 303.

YOU WILL NEED
clean cotton cloths – tea towels, napkins, handkerchiefs
water, to dampen

Take a clean cloth, dampen it with cold water, then lay it out onto a work surface portrait style. Starting at the top, lay two carrots or other veggies side by side and fold over the top and sides. Continue with additional carrots, tucking under the side flaps then rolling the cloth into a huge sausage. I split celery from the head, trim the stalks and roll as for carrots. Don't mix the veggies – make a parcel for each type of veg.

Stored like this in damp towels in the salad compartment of the fridge, your salads, fruit and veggies will keep for weeks rather than days.

Mushrooms – unlike many other fruits and veggies – hate the wet. I don't wash them but simply remove from any packaging, wipe them with dry paper then wrap them in a dry cloth and keep them in the fridge for 10 days to 2 weeks assured shelf-life.

Long-life Lemons and Limes

Inspired by my carrot experiment, I looked for new ways of keep other fruit and veg. This is the best way to keep your citrus fresh.

YOU WILL NEED
glass jars with lids or plastic boxes with lids

Pop lemons and/or limes into a jar or container of cold water after purchase and store in the sealed jar or container in the fridge. They will last for weeks – I kept a lemon for 11 weeks! Renew the water once a week.

TIP: Store limes and lemons separately – I have found that limes lose their colour if kept in the same water as the lemons. Cut lemons and limes keep well too, and a half apple popped into a jar with a half lemon will stay good for at least a week without turning brown.

Lemons do soften in the water, but once left out to dry for an hour or two the skin firms up and they are then suitable for zesting. I have even had social media followers who told me that they rejuvenated their dried-up limes in a jar of water in the fridge – one to try!

Soft Fruits

Soft fruits like strawberries, raspberries and blueberries can be expensive when not in season and a small punnet, once opened, even if kept in the fridge, will start to show signs of deterioration after just two days. This little tip can extend the shelf-life of your fruits for up to two weeks and beyond if they are in season or home grown.

Citric acid is used extensively in food production. This simple acid wash will clean the fruits and destroy any bacteria which otherwise would cause early deterioration of your precious berries. All citric acid is food grade but if your supplies have been purchased specifically for cleaning then the packaging processes may have contaminated your acid. I buy mine in 2kg (4lb 8oz) or 5kg (11lb) bags for both cleaning and food, as it works out cheaper than buying in small 250g (9oz) boxes.

YOU WILL NEED
citric acid, lemon juice or white vinegar
large heatproof bowl
sieve or colander
plastic box or glass jar with lid

Put 10g citric acid (about 2 teaspoons) in a large bowl, add 60ml (2fl oz) boiling water and swirl around until it dissolves and the liquid looks clear. Add 400ml (14fl oz) cold water. Alternatively, use 70ml (2¼fl oz) lemon juice or white vinegar then add 400ml (14fl oz) cold water. I prefer citric acid because there is no residual flavour or odour.

Wash the berries in the solution in batches, swirling them around and using a slotted spoon to remove them and place them in a sieve or colander to drain. Your berries are now cleaned and prepped for a longer, fresher life. There's no need to wash them again before using.

Strawberries with leaves still attached will keep fresher for longer and the leaves should only be removed just before using. Just like tomatoes, they will keep longer with leaves and stalks in place.

If you don't have enough plastic or glass lidded containers, screw-topped glass jars will also keep the soft berries at tip-top condition, but do inspect them regularly (this is easy when they are all visible in a jar): as the fruits are sitting next to each other and are more cramped, if one starts to deteriorate it will start to affect the berry sitting alongside.

CARROT CRISPS

This is a delicious recipe to try, especially if you find yourself with larger-than-average carrots. The carrot shrinks as it dries so what started off as a huge disc ends up being the perfect bite-sized snack.

This recipe makes enough for a large bowl.

YOU WILL NEED
1 or 2 baking sheets
reusable baking parchment or baking paper
food processor with slicer attached, mandoline or sharp
   vegetable knife

2 bumper carrots
2 tbsp oil (sunflower, vegetable, rapeseed, olive)
1 tsp garlic granules (or try paprika, curry powder or ground
   coriander)
salt and pepper

Preheat your oven to 100°C (Gas Mark ¼, 210°F) or pop them into the oven after baking another meal (or have a casserole in the oven at the same time). Line 1 or 2 baking sheets with reusable baking parchment or baking paper (depending on how many carrot slices you yield).

Wash the carrots then top and tail them. Slice the carrots
using a food processor with a slicer attachment or a mandoline,
or slice them thinly by hand using a sharp vegetable knife and
steady hand. Transfer the carrots to a mixing bowl then add
the oil and use your hands to coat the carrots in the oil until
you can see that each slice has a glossy coating. Add the garlic
and/or spices of choice and mix again to coat.

Spread the carrot pieces out on the lined baking sheet(s) in
a single layer, making sure they don't overlap. Bake for about
2 hours, turning them over halfway through. You will know
when the carrots are done as they will be smaller, slightly
wrinkled, yet crispy and tasting gorgeous.

Enjoy this delicious healthy snack just as it is or with a
sprinkle of sea salt flakes. I like to line my serving bowl with
a sheet of crinkled greaseproof paper: as well as making them
look rustic and homemade, this helps absorb any residual oil.
Mine are always eaten in one sitting but if you make lots and
want to keep some for later then an airtight tin or box will
keep them crisp and gorgeous for a week or so.

RHUBARB

No garden or growing space should be without a rhubarb crown. It is the first fresh fruit of the year (even though rhubarb is really a vegetable) and a welcome sight as it lights up the garden with its bright pink stalks. Rhubarb is easy to grow, is a cold weather plant and over the many decades I have grown it I have never had it bothered by pests, bugs or disease. It is a winner in the kitchen too, with many culinary uses, and it is rich in vitamins and antioxidants and considered by some to be a 'super food' because of its health benefits. The leaves, which we don't eat because they contain oxalic acid, can be safely composted. Rhubarb also repels insects, if you're looking for another good reason to have a patch of rhubarb on your veggie plot (see Companion Planting on page 114 for some tips about planning your plot).

Rhubarb grows from early spring and continues to throw out stalks and large leaves until the first frosts in the autumn, though for the crown to continue year upon year it is important not to harvest from midsummer onwards, though it will still need TLC – I come back to this on page 144. Also, if you have a large old rhubarb crown that doesn't perform well it is possible to give it a complete makeover, taking years off its appearance and ensuring that next year you'll be harvesting bumper crops again. I revisit this as a 'job to do' in late autumn (see page 227).

For now, harvest it as you like, though young crowns should not be stripped of every stalk – I have several crowns and take a only few stalks at a time from each plant at the beginning of the season.

When it comes to harvesting, don't be tempted to dive in with a knife, cutting the stalk and leaving a small stub at the base of the crown. Instead, take a hand right to the base of the stalk where it is attached then gently sway the stalk from side to side until it loosens from the crown. The stalk will come away with a flap of skin attached (the stipule). This is perfect as you will not have harmed the plant, there will be no raw stalk that may attract rot or disease and the crown will continue to thrive.

Rhubarb, Orange and Ginger Jam

Rhubarb crumble, rhubarb fool, rhubarb pie… I love them all, though at the start of every season, without fail, I make a batch of jam. I urge you to try it. No thermometer necessary. When I go on to make crumbles, pies and so on, I intensify the fruit flavour by sweetening them with this jam rather than sugar. Two or three tablespoons stirred into 500g (1lb 2oz) raw rhubarb then popped into a pie or crumble will result in a firmer base and more intense fruit flavour. If you make this jam (please do!) you will need to prep the rhubarb the night before, to allow the sugar to dissolve naturally, resulting in less cooking time.

Makes 6 x 450g (1lb) jars

YOU WILL NEED
large casserole or saucepan
grater
2 saucers
wooden spoon

6 x 450g (1lb) clean glass jam jars with screw-top lids
jam funnel (optional)

800g (1lb 12oz) fresh rhubarb (trimmed weight)
1 orange
1kg (2lb 4oz) granulated sugar
60g (2¼oz) preserved stem ginger
4 tbsp liquid pectin (available from the supermarket)

The night before making the jam, cut the rhubarb into 2.5cm (1-inch) lengths and transfer to a large casserole or saucepan. Grate the zest from the orange and add that too.

Segment the orange – remove the top and bottom of the orange with a sharp knife, stand it on a flat board and carefully pare off the layer of pith, working from the top of the orange down to the base, following the shape of the orange. Hold the orange in the palm of one hand and, with a knife in the other hand, carefully remove each segment. Run the knife down each side of each membrane then remove only the flesh part of each segment. You will be left with an orange carcass. Add the orange segments to the pan of rhubarb and squeeze the juice from the carcass into the pan too. (You don't need the carcass for this recipe, but it doesn't have to be wasted, see page 210.) Cut the stem ginger into fine dice and sprinkle it over the fruits, then add the sugar and leave covered in a cool place overnight.

The next day you will notice that most of the sugar has dissolved and the fruits are sitting in a pool of sugar syrup.

When you're ready to make the jam, pop two saucers into the freezer.

Place the pan over a low heat and stir from time to time until the sugar dissolves and doesn't feel gritty when stirred with the wooden spoon. Then, turn up the heat and bring up to a fast boil. Don't stir too often because you will break up the pieces of fruit.

During this time transfer your cold clean glass jars into a cold oven and set the temperature to 100°C (Gas Mark ¼, 210°F). My oven takes about 5–10 minutes to reach this low temperature. Keep the jars in there for 30 minutes, after which time the oven can be turned off (but keep the door closed; any residual heat will keep the jars hot) and the hot jars will be sterilised and ready when we need to jar our jam. I reuse jars and lids but if they have previously been used for pickles you may see that the lids have corroded and started to rust due to the vinegar. Do not reuse these lids. It is possible to buy replacement lids for certain jars. If you are reusing lids that have been used for jams (rather than pickles) in the past, then they will be fine. Wash the lids in warm soapy water then pop them into a small saucepan, cover them with hot water (either from the tap or kettle) and boil for 10 minutes to sterilise.

Back to the jam . . . Boil it for 15 minutes, stirring from time to time to prevent the fruit sticking or burning at the bottom of the pan. As the water in the mixture evaporates, the mixture will start to thicken. The jam will have transformed from a runny mixture to a thicker, slowly bubbling mass. A froth will develop on the surface of the jam which will disappear as the jam cools slightly so don't worry about it. Take the pan off the heat then add the pectin and stir thoroughly, scraping down any jam from the sides of the pan while at the same time thoroughly incorporating the pectin.

To test for a set, put a spoonful onto one of the chilled

saucers and leave to cool or pop it into the fridge for a minute or two. When pushed with a finger, it should wrinkle and be thick; if the jam is still very liquid, bring it to the boil and boil rapidly for another 10 minutes. The jam will thicken as it cools too so err on the side of caution before deciding to boil it some more. It is better to have a slightly runny finished jam than one that has to be cut into slices! When you have achieved a setting jam, transfer into the hot sterilised jars (using a funnel if you like), seal with a lid and leave to go completely cold, then label the jars.

Rhubarb jam spread maybe a little too thickly on warm buttered toast is a springtime treat for me and a sure sign that more home-made jams from other fruits will follow.

MID SPRING

M id spring is my favourite time of year for so many reasons. The days are longer, the sun begins to feel warm, the dawn chorus is the best alarm clock, the spring flowers and blossoms are looking their best, and get close enough and you can see and hear the busy bees visiting every flower. We can step into bright summer clothing on certain days. Oh, and last but no not least, it is the month of my birthday (Primrose Day)! As an aside, do you remember as a child if you were given a diary as a Christmas or birthday gift, the first entry was always your own birthday!

This period of the gardening year I have often seen being referred to as 'The Hungry Gap', those weeks where most of the winter veggies have been harvested yet the current year's harvest is still in its infancy. There are a number of early fresh pickings available such as wild garlic and tender young fresh nettle tips and both will make a great pesto and soup. Nettles are very nutritious and are readily avail-able, though remember to wear gloves for harvesting. Just like spinach, nettles reduce down considerably to about a quarter of their volume during cooking, so har-vest plenty if you can. The sting disappears during cooking. Boil in a small amount of salted water until tender, drain, then serve with ground black pepper and a knob of butter to make a welcome fresh, free food.

Transplanting Sweet Peas

Bushy sweet peas growing well in their tubes or pots, once grown to 10–15cm (6 to 8 inches) in height, can be planted outside and given support to start climbing. Sweet peas are hardy individuals, and a night frost will not harm them now. A pyramid-type construction from canes or thin branches will form a perfect climbing frame, they will scramble up a wall if given a trellis to work to and will – I promise – give you the most gorgeous cut flowers in 8 weeks or so.

Emerging Raspberry Leaves

Bright pale green leaves will be 'poussing' from their buds on canes, whereas autumn varieties will be sending their leaves up straight from the ground. 'Poussing' is a French verb which I think explains exactly what is going on. I don't think we have a word that is quite so descriptive. We could say pushing, sprouting, shooting, bursting, or opening, but 'poussing' is just right. Whatever your favourite word to use, bright vibrant young green leaves are everywhere – this is a wonderful season.

Transplanting Leeks

Once the leeks sown at the start of the season have reached the height and thickness of a drinking straw or thin pencil, they are ready to be transplanted to their final growing space.

There are various methods for doing this and one year there was a slight fuss when I suggested to 'Him Indoors' that he was planting them wrongly. I always trim the tops and the roots you see, but he leaves them as they are! The outcome of this dispute? No difference whatsoever, so choose whichever method suits you.

Choose a day when the weather is likely to turn showery and the ground is also quite moist.

I use a trowel to lift my tiny leeks and tease off the soil from the roots, then I give the roots a haircut to about 5cm (2 inches) long, also cutting back the green tops slightly so that the leek to be transplanted, including the root, is about 30cm (12 inches) tall.

I then mark out my row using my rope and sticks (see page 50) and use a dibber to make a neat hole 15cm (6 inches) deep, drop the root into the hole and then immediately water in with a watering can (known as puddling in). This method of planting ensures the leeks will grow to a decent length below ground as well as above. Once harvested the leek will reveal its full unique beauty of creamy white bottom half and dark green top with thick leaves. Continue planting at 15–20cm (6–8 inch) intervals until all of the infant leeks have been puddled in!

The reason I trim the roots and tops is so they then readily drop into the hole without some long rogue root leaving itself on the surface. The neatened tops too stand upright rather than a long leaf falling limp onto the soil and it is my belief (though I have no evidence to back it up) that the leeks are stimulated after a haircut and will grow big and strong. Alternatively, transplant your leeks without trimming – the results will still be great.

Make sure your transplanted leeks are kept well-watered and weed free and they will be ready to harvest later in the year as either tender youngsters in autumn or fresh from the garden as mature specimens during winter and the following spring.

Nasturtiums

I adore nasturtiums – their flowers, their smell . . . they're edible too and now is the time to sow outside if you haven't started them earlier in pots in a greenhouse or indoors. 'Him Indoors' doesn't care much for nasturtiums so I secretly used to grow them in pots or drop a seed here and there around the garden. He has given up moaning about them now, he knows it's a lost cause. They will grow anywhere – in the hollow of a tree, in the roughest of ground, in hanging baskets and tubs – I love them. I like to use the flowers for cake decorations (see page 76), the leaves in salads and the young buds can be pickled to make mock capers.

They will flower right until the first frosts and will seed themselves too so once you have them, they will appear year after year. They are also a brilliant companion plant and 'sacrificial plant' – offering themselves up to be eaten and nibbled at by bugs thereby protecting your veggies. See Companion Planting on page 114.

WILD GARLIC

I am fortunate to have a small patch of wild garlic leaves at the bottom of my garden which, during spring, are a welcome fresh crop. The plant produces white star-shaped flowers too, which have a subtle garlic flavour and are a great garnish and addition to fresh green salads. Before the flowers appear, the large buds can also be added to pasta, stir-fries, soups and casseroles – they look like capers but have a gorgeous mild garlic flavour. They can be preserved in vinegar to use as mock capers.

When foraging for wild garlic, or in fact any wild edible, it is important not to dig up the whole root or take too many leaves from one plant otherwise it may struggle to thrive then could be lost forever. If you have a shady woody area in your garden, you can buy wild garlic seeds and start off your own patch. It will double in size year on year.

Wild garlic has a short season, though that is part of its joy. It signals the start of spring and the growing season ahead. Although I cannot enjoy the fresh leaves throughout the year, the finely chopped leaves can be stirred through soft butter then frozen in ice cube trays, see page 109.

CAUTION – wild garlic leaves are similar in appearance to Lily of the Valley and grow in the same kind of environment. Lily of the Valley is poisonous so always sniff the leaves before collecting them for food.

Wild Garlic Seasoning

I have managed to capture the colour and flavour of my delicious Wild Garlic in this simple seasoning too and I love to take this to the table in a glass pepper pot. The dark green 'pepper' always raises a few eyebrows.

This dark green powder is beautiful and tastes delicious. Have a go and enjoy the colour and distinct flavour of fresh wild garlic long after the season has passed. I add it to grated cheese, stir it into pasta, add it to stir fries, to roasted vegetables – it has so many uses. Pick dry leaves (not in the morning when they may have a coating of dew or just after rain, because it will make the drying process take much longer).

YOU WILL NEED
2 sheets of kitchen paper
large plate
scissors
microwave
small recycled glass spice or herb jar
food processor

bunch of wild garlic

Cut any thick stalks from the wild garlic leaves (add them to your compost or pop them into a bag and freeze ready to add to another layer of flavour when making stock).

Lay a piece of kitchen paper on a large microwaveable plate then use the scissors to cut the leaves into shreds. Spread the trimmings over the paper, cover with a second sheet of paper then microwave on high for 20 seconds.

Take the plate out of the microwave, remove the top sheet of paper and allow the steam to escape. Fluff up the leaves then cover again and put back into the microwave. This time, turn the wattage down to just 100 watts and set the timer for 30 minutes. Halfway through, fluff the leaves again and cover.

After this time the leaves should be completely dried and crisp. If not, pop them back in the microwave for a further 5–10 minutes. Once the leaves are dried and cooled down, blitz to a powder in the small bowl of a food processor – transfer to the glass jar and enjoy.

TIP: Drying home-grown herbs in this way, and storing them in old glass supermarket herb and spice jars will keep the kitchen stocked and save money. Thyme, basil, mint, parsley, chives, sage, tarragon, dill – all dry beautifully using this method.

SEASONAL SPECIAL –
NATURAL CAKE DECORATIONS

I simply had to include this tip in honour of my springtime birthday. Primroses are edible flowers, as are daisies, violets, dandelions, nasturtiums, wild garlic, chive and elderflowers.

Magnolia petals too, they taste like a kind of floral cucumber. I use many edible flowers in salads and cake decorations along with young and bright green, fresh mint leaves.

Primroses in particular look beautiful when crystallised and, once dried, will keep for months in an airtight box in a cool, dark place. One Instagram follower used these directions to decorate her wedding cake – it looked absolutely stunning. Crystallised primroses retain their shape and colour and when made using a home-made vanilla sugar make a tasty sweet edible natural and nearly free cake decoration.

This mix will crystallise as many as 25–30 flowers

YOU WILL NEED
small scissors
small bowl
mini whisk
small paint brush
chopping board
teaspoon
tweezers
kitchen paper and fine-mesh tray

fresh primroses (or other edible flowers)
1 egg white
50g (1¾oz) caster sugar (or try vanilla caster sugar, see tip
    page 79)

I only cut the primroses when I am ready to crystallise so they are as fresh as can be – a wilted flower will not crystallise well and may not be strong enough to hold up to the treatment.

Cut the flowers, leaving only a small stalk to make them easier to handle. It is better to cut the flowers in the morning before they have seen the sun and when the weather is dry. I choose the flowers that are clean from my garden, not dirt-splattered or water marked. I don't bother to wash them but if you want to wash them before crystallising, do this carefully as they easily bruise and discolour. After washing, make sure they are dried off face down on kitchen paper before starting. Even better – if you want to crystallise the edibles from your garden, I would wash them while they are still attached to the plant using a fine rose watering can of clean water. Pick them once they have dried off naturally in the fresh air – they will then be 'as fresh as a daisy'; not damaged, bruised or spoilt in any way.

Put the egg white in a small bowl and whisk until just frothy – the white is then easier to paint on, being non-stretchy. Put the sugar in a separate bowl.

Hold the primrose by the stalk in one hand and a paint brush dipped in egg white in the other. Begin by gently laying the flower face down on a chopping board. Paint the underside of each petal individually, making sure to cover the surface with a thin layer of egg white. Still holding the flower by the stalk, lift the flower and paint the top side of the petals and the flower's centre.

Once coated, and still holding onto the stalk, face-plant the flower into the bowl of sugar. Use a teaspoon to flick sugar grains over the underside of the petals then cut off the stalk at the receptacle (the part where the stalk joins the flower) and cover the whole lot with sugar.

Once the whole bloom has a sugar coating, gently lift from the sugar using tweezers then transfer to a sheet of kitchen paper laid over a fine mesh tray, and place it face down. Laying the flower face down retains the shape. Leave on a work surface at room temperature until dried out.

To know whether the flowers have crystallised, pick one up and they will feel hard and brittle. Once completely dried they can be stored in an airtight box or tin in a cool place. These flowers will keep for months and months (I know, because I came across a box one Christmas which had been leftovers from a cake I had made the previous spring. I munched on one or two and they were absolutely fine, though they're obviously much better made fresh!).

They're a great natural beautiful cake, chocolate and dessert decoration.

||||||||||||||||||||||||||||||||||||||||||||||||||||||||||||||||||||||||||||||||||||||||||||||||||||||||||||||||

TIP: Vanilla pods are very expensive so I try to make sure I use every morsel. Once the seeds have been scraped away and used in custards, creams, baked crème caramel and brûlée, rather than discarding the pod, cut it into three inch or so lengths. Pop the dried dark brown pieces into a clean glass jar, topping up with caster sugar as you go so that they are well distributed then on with the lid. Leave to infuse for about a week and the next time you unscrew the jar you will have a delicious vanilla smelling and tasting caster sugar – perfect for baking, crystallising or simply sprinkling over your fresh strawberries in summer. Leave the pod pieces in the jar and top up with sugar again and again.

||||||||||||||||||||||||||||||||||||||||||||||||||||||||||||||||||||||||||||||||||||||||||||||||||||||||||||||||

SEEDS: THE THREE PS

For the novice gardener, examine the details on the reverse of seed packets and you will be given instructions as to whether your seeds can be sown straight into the ground at this time of year or need to be sown in trays or pots and kept indoors. Some packets will even tell you the approximate temperature the seeds will require to germinate.

The veggies that can be sown straight into the ground includes crops such as peas, spinach, radishes, carrots, parsnips, swedes and beetroot. Once these have germinated, the little seedlings need to be **pinched out**, thereby removing the weaker of the plants and giving the stronger crops room to expand.

Not all veggies planted straight into the ground need to be pinched out. The larger seeds of peas and broad beans can be planted exactly where you want them to grow.

Other veggies, such as cabbages, cauliflowers, broccoli and sprouts, had you wanted to get ahead, would have been sown in trays or pots in early spring and kept indoors, to be planted out later as the weather warms up. Such seeds, sown last month, may now be ready to **prick out**. This is the term given to separating tiny seedlings and giving them more space to grow.

Then there's the **planting out**, which is the last stage when the seeds that were sown in trays or pots and maybe kept indoors are given their final growing space – whether that be in the ground or a container. Let us refer to them as 'The Three Ps' for Seeds. Already we are embracing a brand-new garden vocabulary!

Pinching Out

This term applies to seeds that have been sown directly into the ground, in particular those very small ones which are nearly impossible to single out at sowing time. The seed packet will explain how deep the seed has to be sown and how far apart the final spacing has to be.

Let us say, for example, we are dealing with sowing a row of beetroot (though as mentioned this method will also be applied to parsnips, carrots and spinach). The seeds of beetroot resemble minute nuts and are quite easy to handle compared to some others. The packet will say that the final amount of space a beetroot needs is 10cm (4 inches). I plant these seeds about 1cm (½ inch) apart in a row about 1cm (½ inch) deep.

As these seeds are an easy-to-handle size and the packet says that each beetroot needs 10cm (4 inches) to itself, then you may ask why not just plant one seed every 10cm (4 inches) – surely that is more cost effective? The trouble is, nature makes up its own mind and some years every seed will germinate – which is great – but other years, maybe only 50 per cent. By sowing at 1cm (½ inch) intervals, I am pretty certain I will achieve a good row. In addition, just like all living things – not every seedling is going to be as fit and strong as the one next door.

A couple of weeks after sowing the seeds at 1cm (½ inch) intervals I can see that all the seeds that are going to germinate have germinated and once the little plants stand 5–7.5cm (2–3 inches) tall I can examine the row and remove – pinch out – the weakest, thereby leaving more space and more soil nutrients for those remaining.

My initial observations are that part of the row may look cluttered, whereas further along there may be fewer – had I not sown so many I will have had barren gaps in the row. I start by 'pinching out' to 5cm (2 inches) apart. This involves working steadily along the row, carefully examining the row of red stalks, taking hold of the smallest at ground level and gently easing them out. I leave the strongest and tallest plants 5cm (2 inches) apart while carefully pulling out the neighbours.

I like to do this job just before a rain shower because any soil disturbance is soon backfilled and rectified once the rain or a watering can has re-settled the soil around the remaining plants.

I will repeat the exercise in a month or so and do the final 'pinch' to 10cm (4 inches) between each beetroot plant then leave them to reach maturity in mid to late summer.

||||||||||||||||||||||||||||||||||||||||||||||||||||||||||||||||||||||||||||||||||||||||||||||||||||||||||||||||||||||||||||||||||||||||||||

TIP: Add pinched-out veggie seedlings to your salads, just snip off the roots first.

||||||||||||||||||||||||||||||||||||||||||||||||||||||||||||||||||||||||||||||||||||||||||||||||||||||||||||||||||||||||||||||||||||||||||||

Pricking Out

This is the term that I apply to those seeds that have been sown into trays or small containers. The seeds may have been very small and had been simply scattered over a layer of compost that has been filled to a depth of about 2.5–5cm (1–2 inches) in a tray and covered with a fine layer of compost, watered and then left to grow. Cabbages, cauliflowers, kale, broccoli, lettuce, parsley, coriander and basil are a few examples of the seeds I start in trays and then prick out. Huge seeds such as those of sweetcorn, beans, courgettes, cucumbers and aubergines I plant directly into their own small pots, thereby skipping the 'pricking out' stage.

When the seeds have germinated, the tray will be dotted with tiny pairs of bright green leaves. This is so exciting – take satisfaction that you are doing everything right. Often, however, enthusiastic novice growers then begin to overdo things a bit – and I have certainly done this myself. Too much heat and the seedlings will grow too tall (looking leggy), with long stems and tiny leaves. Also, not enough light will encourage the seedlings to grow tall looking and searching for bright light – the leaves will turn pale, the stalk long and spindly, and eventually, feeling completely worn out and fed up, they'll fall over and collapse.

Try to remember that once the seedlings have produced their first tiny pair of leaves that will be sitting just above the ground they need to be kept moist, warm and given LOTS of light and then when the second set of leaves has emerged – (their true leaves) which will probably look quite different to the first set – then we can start to **prick out**. It's a bit like our first and second sets of teeth – most baby teeth look the same, but once our adult teeth come through we develop an identity.

For those growing for the first time it can be expensive to go out and buy new plant pots for pricking out. The established gardener or grower will have many pots that have been used and reused over many years. Some garden centres will give away used pots but, failing that, there are many everyday containers and pots that can be recycled and used as perfect growing pots.

YOU WILL NEED

7.5cm (3 inch) pots, which can include: plastic plant pots or terracotta pots

300ml (10fl oz) yoghurt pots

300ml (10fl oz) cream pots

bottom half of a plastic milk container

compost

a pencil

plant labels – make your own from lolly sticks or cut up plastic pots (see page 247)

marker pen (or use the pencil)

a large wooden tray or a plastic lid or tray to work on so that compost spills can be gathered up and popped back into the bag after the job is finished

In addition to the above, any other tub-type plastic container around 7.5cm (3 inches) in diameter and depth can be used. Wash your pots, create a number of drainage holes in the base (I use a hot metal skewer or simply the pointed end of a knife) and you have the perfect plant pot for your new babes.

Pricking out is fairly straight-forward, I find it very relaxing. I have the radio on in the shed or greenhouse or instead just listen to the birds singing in the background.

Using the pencil, take the pointed end and use it to gently loosen the compost around and underneath the bed of seedlings. Their network of roots will have mingled together but by easing a pencil underneath, the web is loosened and the little plants will let go of their neighbours when you are ready to lift them out.

I then fill my pot with compost (home-made if you have it but more often than not it will need to be bought, see page 24). There is such a huge variety of brightly coloured compost bags to choose from which will suit all plant types. I tend to say that any peat-free general-purpose compost will do. It can all get very detailed and complicated, so go for a mid-price multi-purpose. I say mid-price because one year I decided to opt for the very cheapest on offer to try it out. For me this was a bad decision: the seedlings quickly turned yellow, suggesting a lack of nutrients, the compost seemed to contain huge clumps which refused to crumble and, even worse, there were non-rotted pieces of wood present which made it very difficult for seedlings to get a strong hold. It didn't retain water at all and quickly dried out. I had to go out and buy a mid-price compost and quickly transplant the seedlings in order to save them from an early grave. Have you heard the old saying 'I am not rich enough to buy cheap goods'? You know me by now and I love a bargain. There are lots of places where you can save but this example ended up costing me more!

Leaf mould and/or your own compost can be used for growing your seedlings too or a mix of all three (bought, leaf mould, home compost). I have had excellent results using a mixed combo.

Once the pots are filled it is necessary to gently firm the compost down. A good compost is light and airy and the pot may look full to the brim so gently press it slightly then add more to fill right to the top so that the new plants have compost rather than air pockets to enjoy. If the compost is not compressed lightly before planting then the first time your new plant is watered, the compost will settle down and your pot will look just half full.

With a full pot of compost at the ready I use the stub pencil end to form a little planting hole in the centre. Now to remove the seedling. An important note is to pick the seedling up gently and tease it out of the compost using the pencil in one hand and the seedling leaf between thumb and forefinger in the other hand. If the seedling is healthy there will be a good network of roots going on. If the leaf is to get damaged or at worst torn the seedling will still survive – if, however, the seedling is being handled by the stem and it gets bent or damaged, the seedling will die.

Once you've managed to separate your seedling from its siblings it can be carried over to the ready-made spacious new home with cupboards full of food. Simply lower the roots into the hole and firm up the compost around the stem. A good watering after pricking out is essential using the fine rose of a watering can (not a heavy-handed hosepipe). Then simply watch them grow until they are ready for the next stage – Planting Out or Potting On!

Planting Out or Potting On

What started off as a tender seedling in a 7.5cm (3 inch) pot after several weeks of care and attention will be probably around 7.5–10cm (3–4 inches) in height, bushy and healthy looking. The seedlings that were 'pricked out' or sown last month will be ready to **plant out** during late spring and, fingers crossed, by the end of the season it should also be the end of any frost.

If you have been growing young plants in a greenhouse or on a windowsill, rather than moving them straight away into their new growing position in the garden or an outside pot, give them a few days to get used to things. Remember these young plants have been rather spoilt – they have been kept warm, given a fine spray of water regularly and have had a good supply of sun on their backs. There has been no wind to rock them from side to side and they've not had any of the rough stuff that the true outdoors brings. The plants need to be 'hardened off', a term given to acclimatising young plants to the outdoors. Simply pop your trays or pots of young plants outside during the day, bringing them in at night for 3 to 4 days then leaving them out day and night for 3–4 days. About a week of gently adjusting the plants to the outdoors means that once in the ground, the shock of moving from a comfy warm pot to the great outdoors will be greatly reduced.

Some plants such as beans, sweetcorn and courgettes will be ready to plant outside, but if you have limited space and find that you haven't yet got any room – perhaps you're waiting for potatoes or autumn-planted onions to ripen – don't panic. Offer your plants a bigger pot which will keep them going for several more weeks until their permanent bed is ready. I routinely do this with courgettes and sweetcorn.

Many crops are more than happy to spend their whole time in a pot – the plant being potted on to a larger vessel as it grows. Some growers will raise a whole range of veggies and fruits only in containers. I grow lots of basil plants in 15cm (6 inch) pots and tomatoes, aubergines, sweet peppers, chillies and cucumbers in large 30cm (12 inch) pots and my Luffa plants occupy large 40cm (16 inch) pots. Growing in pots ensures you can move plants around and choose the best sunny yet sheltered position outside, on a patio or 'under glass' in a greenhouse.

Pot-grown sweet peppers are very easy. If looked after – kept warm, well-watered, given a cane support as they grow tall, and a weekly feed of half-strength organic tomato feed – each plant will produce between 6 and 8 super fruits. A good year will yield many colourful gorgeous peppers.

Chillies especially make a great indoor plant if you have a conservatory or very sunny room. They will stand happily on a sunny windowsill and, unlike tomato or cucumber plants, will remain compact and well-shaped. A bushy plant bearing white flowers followed by green pods then the brightest red chilli fruits in the autumn can look a spectacle as an 'edible' house plant. There are many varieties to choose from too – bell shaped, scotch bonnet, green, yellow, very hot to very mild. One plant can yield many fruits which can be popped straight into the freezer to keep you supplied and used from frozen or used to make a chilli sauce – see page 199.

Before deciding to 'plant out' or 'pot on', examine the roots of your plants. To do this simply secure the main growing stem of your plant between forefinger and middle finger of one hand

and turn the pot upside down, thereby resting the surface of the compost in the palm with the plant suspended below. Remove the pot and examine the roots which should be filling the pot and indicating to you that it is time to move on to bigger premises. If, however, the compost is still not being occupied by a network of roots, best to leave it another week or two to allow the plant to further establish itself.

Lifting off a pot to see what is going on in the plant's engine room is always fascinating. A plant's leaves may look a little pale, it may seem to dry out quickly or, alternatively, it may appear perfectly happy on the surface. However, when the roots inside the pot are observed you may be shocked to see that the soil or compost has been just about all used up, the roots have taken up the whole space, winding around and around the pot, some thick, some thin but clearly this plant needs a bigger growing space. When a plant is 'root bound' in this way, before potting on I tend to tease some of those roots apart to just help the transition and point the roots into the right direction away from the centre of the root ball into new compost.

There are plants that perform really well when root bound, namely figs and orchids, so don't be in any hurry to repot these. I am no orchid expert, though I used to have a fig tree (which unfortunately didn't survive a very cold winter) but if you have ever seen huge fig trees growing wild, they will seem to be flourishing on very little or poor ground, maybe on the edge of a stony bank or a dry crack in an old wall – amazing. When I planted a fig tree I constructed a concrete vessel from 4 concrete pavers below ground so that the roots would be restricted thereby encouraging it to bear more fruits. As I am writing I feel nostalgic about my fig tree so will add planting a new one to my plan for next year!

SOWING OUTDOORS

As the weather warms up many seeds can be sown directly into the soil. Seed packets will give all the information required about spacing, depth, height, etc., but as a general rule I wait until the end of this season to sow my seeds (especially peas) directly into the ground even though I am being told by the packet I can sow earlier.

The reason for this is that I seem to have a 'love-hate' relationship with peas. I love them but they do seem to give me the run-around in years gone by and this is the way I've found yields the highest success rate. If you have struggled with peas failing to germinate, try holding out before planting to make sure the soil is going to stay warm.

So many times, I have sown them outside during a mild spell early in the season, which was then followed by a wet, cold snap causing some of the peas to rot in the ground resulting in little or no germination. It's one of the most difficult decisions, try not to give in to temptation to plant early.

Your seed packet will offer a two- or three-month sowing window and the temptation is to dive in as soon as the weather is warm, the birds are singing and you are enjoying being outside. A packet may advise sowing mid spring – it may be very early in the season and after due consideration you are going to sow the seeds. The packet says it is fine so in they go. As described, the weather then turns, and you wonder whether things will ever warm up again. Your seeds are feeling exactly the same and maybe only a few will germinate and survive. Much better to hang on a few weeks and be more confident about the weather. It is spring after all. I have had as many snow showers on my birthday in April as I have non-jumper days.

It is far easier for shoots to catch up in perfect growing conditions after being sown later in the season rather than having to suffer a stunted or hard start due to cold or wet conditions following your early sowing.

Seeds such as runner beans, French beans and courgettes can be started off quite safely in pots in mid spring. They will germinate quickly under glass or on a sunny windowsill and can then be transplanted after the risk of frost at the end of the season.

A note on beans for the container grower: all beans grow well in pots and a number of runner beans grown in a large pot – after having been given a pyramid framework of 3 or 5 tall canes 1.5 metres (5 foot) or 1.8 metres (6 foot) high, secured at the top with string – will provide a tall imposing colourful display during mid and late summer. The crimson flowers as well as the beans pods and – later on in the season – the colourful beans are all edible and I believe every grower should enjoy this easy crop. Resistant to disease, it doesn't attract pests, is easy to grow and provides lots and lots!

Sow one bean seed per 7.5cm (3 inch) pot – they are very well behaved when it comes to germination – and leave on a sunny windowsill or greenhouse until germination takes place – this will usually take about 10 days. Once they plants are 7.5–10cm (3–4 inches) (see Potting On page 87), the bean plants can be transferred, 3 or 4 per pot, to a large 30cm (12 inch) pot and offered a cane for each plant.

SPRING FLOWERING BULBS

From mid-season onwards – depending on weather conditions – beds, tubs and planters of early daffodils may start to fade. I recall that many years ago my grandad used to remove the faded blooms then tie the leaves in tiny parcels with string, leaving them to die down naturally. I have to say I don't bother dead-heading all of my daffodils in garden beds for three reasons: firstly, I have too many, secondly, I recall reading somewhere that while it is necessary to dead-head tulips, daffodils don't mind being left to die back naturally, and thirdly, it is a time-consuming and back-breaking job. Oh, and there's a fourth – I still get flowers the following year even though I have done no dead-heading whatsoever.

I make an exception though, and that is for my daffodils and other flowering bulbs growing in pots and planters. I regularly dead-head these because they are the bulbs I will lift and split later on in the year (see page 166) and use to plant up even more pots for next spring. Dead-heading will ensure flowers next year, whereas leaving them be is more of a lottery.

Once my tubs and planters are looking floppy, with the flowers gone yet still lots of green leaves, I move them to an out-of-the-way place in the garden where I continue to water them until the leaves have turned brown.

I realise some readers will want to use the same planters for summer bedding flowers and I have some favourite planters that I want to use for summer too. We can do one of two things – either leave the dead-headed bulbs in the planters where they are and at the end of next season add more compost to the tub and plant young summer bedding plants over the top. The bulbs will come again next spring, or water the tubs well then gently lift the clumps of bulbs from the pot, taking as much compost with them as you can – the compost will cling to the bulbs if it is moist. Take the clumps of bulbs and pop them into a 'holding bed' in the garden to finish dying off. We can then revisit them in late summer (see page 166).

WEEDS

Weeds – or should I say – 'anything that is growing in a place where you don't want it to', will start to take a hold in spring as the sun shines, there are regular rain showers and growing conditions are perfect.

Around the garden I have become fairly tolerant of weeds, as so many have culinary uses. Dandelions and nettles, for example, are very nutritious and will bulk out basil when making home-made pesto. However, on the veggie plot I am strict and keep the weeds at bay as best I can. I want every morsel of goodness and moisture in my ground to feed my veggies, not provide extra strength to a group of weeds that have moved in and have started to raid the cupboards.

In dry weather, the top leaves of weeds can be chopped off with a hoe which stops them in their tracks and will control some but the toughies will recover and come back bigger and better. In damp conditions it is better to pull them out root and all, and this is easier to do when the weeds are young and the soil is damp following a good downpour.

I actually enjoy a veggie plot weeding day when the conditions are just perfect. I like the ground to be moist, the sun to be shining then I get on all fours, start at one end and simply weave myself up and down the rows. I have a large bucket and a hand trowel. I am up close with my veggies and at the same time can keep a keen eye on their well-being.

Raised beds and pots are easier to weed and to make access to my veggies simple I have created 'well-trodden' pathways between each growing area which enables me to weed, hoe, harvest, prick out and plant out without having to walk over the actual beds. The soil of growing areas doesn't then become compacted and hard and is therefore very easy to weed.

Troublesome weeds that appear in paths and patios can be controlled quickly, cheaply and effectively – in fact, I have found they don't come back at all and most importantly we are doing less harm to our precious planet. Rather than purchasing weed killers or path clearing products, many of which are harmful to aquatic life, and often promise to control weeds for only just one season – pour over boiling water straight from the kettle followed immediately by a light sprinkle of table salt. That's it! Any troublesome weeds are gone forever.

LATE SPRING

The Swifts arrive, squealing with delight and adding to the cacophony of other bird sounds. By the end of spring, we hope to have had the last of any frost, though there are always those seasons that go on to break the rules. I recall on one spring bank holiday running out with pieces of used compost bags to cover up tender young geranium plants to protect them from a 'minus 5' frost forecast that night. The geraniums survived, but the tips on the lower leaves of my runner beans were damaged and turned brown, though all was not lost – they survived and went on to provide good crops.

Generally, we can sow and plant safely outdoors in late spring without the need for extra protection, though, just to be on the safe side, I continue to protect tender plants such as tomatoes sitting in pots outdoors with my plastic box at night until they become accustomed to the great outdoors and have grown too tall for the box.

Sow runner beans and French beans in pots and boxes if they have not been started off indoors already. Salads too can be sown straight into pots and containers.

If you have a sunny spot, a small greenhouse or cold frame, then try sowing aubergines, sweet peppers and chillies now. They are such fun to grow. I always have them in pots rather than in the ground and they will crop well in late summer and early autumn if nurtured and kept warm.

Those who have lawns and grassy areas may be mowing weekly, increasing to nearly twice a week (for the very keen!) by the next season. I have to say my garden is not as manicured or nearly as formal as it used to be with neat edges and closely mown grass. I have a number of areas I simply leave to nature with a mown path running through. This encourages insect populations and in so many ways is more natural, beautiful and interesting – and less work!

I occasionally use an organic fertiliser to treat the lawn and am happy to add the clippings to the compost. If you have lots of grass clippings to add to the compost, spread them in thin layers, adding paper, cardboard or dried leaves in between to prevent them clogging into a thick smelly mess – see page 34 and remember, think 'triple decker' club sandwich.

Try to resist the temptation to tidy up hedges and bushes with shears and hedge trimmers. It is important to wait until midsummer as birds will be nesting, raising their babes and teaching them the ways of the world. They are very careful when choosing a quiet, well-hidden spot but will be frightened off, never to return to their young if the keen gardener comes up close and personal with a loud destructive power tool.

By late spring the whole garden, planting area, balcony or window box is coming to life. The garden centres are bursting with tempting colours and displays. The container gardener can begin to show off – the new planting will be adding height, colour, interest, beauty and, more to the point, nutritional healthy home-grown food too!

The message really to anyone starting out is have a go – pop a strawberry plant in a pot, drop a few nasturtium seeds in a hollow of a tree, sprinkle salad seeds into a window box, start a small herb garden in plastic milk-bottle bases (after making drainage holes in the base). Any gardener will be happy to hand over small cuttings, surplus seedlings and leftover seeds and of course some of what is growing wild or in the hedgerow can be eaten too.

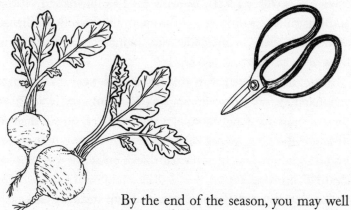

By the end of the season, you may well have the first sign of flowers on tomato plants both indoors and outdoors, and a mini harvest of salad leaves and radishes. Plant out parsley and rocket that may have been grown from seed, anywhere in the garden ready to snip a few leaves later on when you need them.

Planting Veggies

Towards the end of the season, beans not already started off in pots inside can be planted straight into the ground. The soil is warming up and germination will take place quickly.

As well as sowing them in a prepared seed bed I have grown both French beans and runner beans in containers, pots and boxes with great results and they are veggies I would thoroughly recommend to any gardener – one plant will give a good crop, they are great for freezing, and delicious eaten raw or cooked.

This season will probably be your main sowing time for veggies so whatever you are wanting to grow, check the packets, check your quick reference crop guide (see pages 257 and 298). If you want to get going and skip a step, you will find small trays of vegetable plants available for sale in garden centres and supermarkets – it's even better if you link up with friends: they may well have planted more than they can manage in their own gardens.

I have an arrangement with a friend each year – I exchange a number of my home-grown tomato plants and she grows the most amazing Cosmos for me from seed. This is a great division-of-labour arrangement and if you have a network of friends who are keen gardeners, what a great low-cost way to start the growing season.

Towards the end of the season, you will certainly pick up a bargain as growers will drastically reduce the price of small trays of seedling cabbages, cauliflowers, sprouts, beans – the lot really!

Sowing Courgettes

Courgettes are a fantastic, high-yielding crop and great for the starter gardener. Sow 2 seeds per 7.5cm (3 inch) pot then move onto bigger pots once they've germinated. If you are successful and achieve two plants, once they are 7–10cm (3–4 inches) tall, give them each a 20cm (8 inch) pot of their own. A courgette plant will keep you supplied from midsummer right until the first frosts. A healthy courgette plant can provide as many as 50 fruits.

The bright yellow flowers are edible too and home growing means there is absolutely no need source them from expensive fine food specialists. There are many recipes that use courgette flowers. They are often stuffed with cheese and lemon, then steamed or fried or are simply eaten raw in salads. I like to harvest an immature courgette with the flower still attached, fry in a little sesame oil on both sides until just coloured and serve just as they are, topped with freshly ground black pepper.

Snip Strawberry Stolons

Beautiful colourful displays can be produced in planters of all kinds. Hanging baskets are beautiful and can add to your kitchen's food supply; trailing tomato plants grow well in a sunny spot in hanging baskets or wall mounted pots, and strawberries too grow very well in this way because the fruits do not get damaged when it rains, the birds don't seem to worry them at all and slugs and snails I think find it too much of an 'uphill' struggle to reach them. Strawberries grown in beds will need some protection if you are to enjoy them rather than the birds. I have a simple netted frame which comes out each year and can be easily lifted for harvesting.

I grew a number of strawberry plants in wall-mounted pots. They looked so gorgeous and received many more 'oohs' and 'ahs' than the strawberries in the ground. Trouble is, they looked so beautiful, an absolute picture, that I was reluctant to harvest them – though I did!

Keep an eye on strawberry plants at this

time, whether you are growing them in pots or in their bed. As they excitedly grow new leaves from the tiny crown at the centre, you may also see a rogue 'runner' (stolon) growing out from the centre of the plant. These long stolons, with a bunch of tiny leaves at the end, are the strawberry's way of multiplying and will happen at a fast pace once the strawberries have fruited in summer. However, if you spot a stolon being formed this early, cut it off with scissors. At this early stage you want all energy to go into producing flowers and berries not more plants.

Sow Corn

Sweetcorn sown now will germinate in no time, giving the best-tasting cobs in late summer. I save cardboard tubes for sweetcorn or plant into small pots, sowing the seeds as I did for sweet peas (see page 287) then planting them straight into the ground later when the plants are around 20cm (8 inches) tall. If space for growing is limited, these plants can be transplanted into bigger 13cm (5 inch) pots and will be happy to continue their growing for the next few weeks to be popped into the ground later when broad beans or early potatoes have been harvested. I used to believe sweetcorn was difficult to grow and not really suited to the UK climate, but crops over recent years have been tremendous.

Dead-heading

You may see the first rose blooms, geraniums and petunias appear and – if you are lucky – the first of your sweet pea flowers. To keep them flowering for longer, I remove faded blooms. I apply this to most flowers in the garden and any flowers I have growing in pots. I cut off faded flowers to prevent seed pods forming, resulting in more blooms and a longer flowering period. Pop faded blooms into the compost bin.

Retrain Sweet Peas

Sweet peas should be scrambling to the top of their frame, filling out and looking green, vibrant and healthy. However, keep an eye out for a plant that may be scrambling across the ground, having failed to get a good hold onto the frame that you provided. Pick it up and gently weave it into place. Plants will be around 0.6 metres (2 feet) tall by the end of spring or even taller – you may even see the beginnings of a flower stalk or two. Keep them well watered if the weather is dry, though we hope that late spring gives us lots of rain.

Weed the Potatoes

The First Early potatoes will be bright green bushy plants now about 24cm (10 inches) tall. Don't be tempted to have a look underneath – they'll not be ready until early summer (not long to wait). Keep them well watered if the weather is very dry. It is important to keep your potato plants 'earthed up' and weed free. Hand-weed the rows and ensure the earthed-up mound is still intact and has not been scratched up or dug up by visiting cats or birds. A young developing potato not covered with earth and exposed to the light will turn green and then be inedible.

Green potatoes need to be taken seriously. I have mentioned this earlier in the book but will mention again to make sure – the green colour appears when the potato has been exposed to light. The potato has produced chlorophyll which itself is completely harmless but also signals the presence of toxins which cause the potatoes to taste bitter and makes them dangerous to eat.

Support your Runner Beans

If you decide to grow runner beans (and I recommend you do) then – whether you are growing them in a large pot or a row in the garden – construct the frame first. For the container gardener a large pot filled with compost then a tall frame of about 6 to 8 canes or sticks (1.5–1.8 metres/5–6 feet high) placed in a pyramid shape then secured at the top with string will offer your bean plants an instant support. The plants should be 15–20cm (6–8 inches) tall when planted outdoors and into their final position and see how quickly they begin to wrap themselves around the canes or sticks. By constructing the frame first there is no danger of damaging the roots which could well be the case if the frame is constructed after the plants have been planted into the soil.

Protect Peas and Mangetout

Peas have given me the run-around over the years! A bumper crop one year may then be followed by a feeble show the next year and I have no idea why. The variety of seed may be the same, the way I grow them has been the same – the only variable I cannot control is the weather and I have found that the later the sowing, the better the crop. I don't sow until the mid to late spring now, even though I have been tempted on so many occasions when the weather has been gorgeous.

Young pea shoots will disappear overnight if they are not

netted off from the birds. I can understand the attraction – young pea shoots taste delicious. Wire netting, a purpose-built frame or even a number of coloured plastic bottle tops threaded on a length of string and suspended over the row will deter the birds as they sway around in the breeze. Some gardeners pop the pea-growing sticks into the ground at the time of sowing but my peas are taken by the birds, so I start them off under a protective net then add the sticks later.

Once the peas have reached around 10–15cm (4–6 inches) in height, they go on to grow thin tendrils which is the signal to you that they need to be given climbing supports. By this time the birds have found more interesting shoots to nibble and will leave your peas alone. Remove the nets, bottle tops or frames and replace with canes or – even better – twigs. I save twigs, collecting them during the year (especially in the winter when the winds have snapped a few off) and piling them up alongside the compost bin to be used for this very purpose. They're cheaper than canes and much more effective. The best are those with a few curly branches that can be popped into the ground, offering great support for the peas as they cling on and continue to flourish.

You will see the leaves get bigger and the straight tendrils on the plants will wrap themselves around the supports you have given. There is no need to tie the peas to the twigs – simply lay the plant onto the twig or cane. If not given support, the peas will simply wrap around each other resulting in a tangled mess so as soon as you see the tendrils – it's important you get the sticks out.

I love stories – and this one is true! One spring evening I did just this. I had removed the bird protector and inserted my twigs along the row – one twig or even two per plant. The tendrils were probably 2.5–5cm (1–2 inches) long and straight.

The next morning – so only about twelve hours later – the tendrils which had been straight thin lengths of green string were now wrapped around the twigs so tightly and not just once but over and over and over, hugging so tight that the plant was secure and ready to continue its journey upwards and onwards. So quick, so clever and no overlapping of the tendrils either – neat and tidy! Like a coil of ships' ropes.

Cherish Chives

Chives, with their subtle mild onion flavour, will grow back every year. They are easy to manage and will grow happily in a plant pot outside (it is too warm for them inside).

As well as growing for you year on year they are varied too. They produce dark green spears of fresh mild-flavoured love-liness that I use in so many dishes from spring onwards. They're perfect for topping off jacket potatoes, using in herb butters (see page 109), sprinkling over quiche before baking, garnishing soups and stews – the variations are endless. Not only does the chive give us green – the exciting little purple buds in spring can be harvested as they are and added to pasta, pizza toppings and salads, or can be left and will open up as pale lilac edible flowers looking similar to clover. These can be pulled apart and the little flecks of mild onion flavour can be eaten raw in salads or used as a garnish.

Once the flowers have faded at the end of this season, don't be fooled into thinking that your harvest of chives is finished for the year. Even though your patch of chives may look forlorn, with limp thickened leaves yellowing at the ends and hard tough flower stalks – your supply, though interrupted for a week or so, will soon be back into full production.

Simply take a pair of sharp scissors in one hand and in the other hold together every wilted strand and cut to within about 5cm (2 inches) of the ground: a thorough haircut. Compost the debris, water the stubble and leave the neatly trimmed chives for about a week. Astonishingly in no time you will be delighted to see new small dark green spears poking up from the base and in a week or so you will be clipping and enjoying fresh chives again right up until the first frosts – no more buds or flowers though. Every home should have a pot of chives, then the supermarkets would not need to stock the plastic packs. Spring pickings can also be harvested and dried for winter use (see page 133).

EAT THE THINNINGS!

In spring, even though growing is vigorous and plants are thriving, there may be little to actually munch on just yet, though a fresh plate of veggies can be achieved ahead of time if we eat our thinnings.

When planting out cabbages, sprouts, kale and cauliflowers, for example, the seed packet will advise to plant 30–46cm (12–18 inches) apart but I double them up and plant 15cm (6 inches) apart. As these young brassicas quickly start to grow, I then go in and harvest the weaker plants to use as fresh greens rather than have to go out to buy imported fresh produce from the supermarket.

I have to say the leaves from young plants are so tender and delicious they need very little cooking. I tend to wash the leaves, shred them, then either simply stir-fry or cook in as little as 1cm (½ inch) of water with some salt and a knob of butter. After 1–2 minutes they are wilted, still vibrantly green and taste unbelievable. I never cover home-grown veggies in water for boiling, whatever their age. Just 1cm (½ inch) of boiling water in a pan with a little salt – pop the leaves in, on with a lid and they're sufficiently steamed in a jiffy. This method uses less fuel too – there's no large pan of water brought to the boil and no stodgy 'boiled to their death' veggies being served up.

Apply the same principle to the tender young thinnings from beetroot, turnips, parsnips and radishes. As these crops grow you will want to remove the weaker, more feeble plants thereby allowing the strong specimens more space to grow.

Rather than tossing them onto the compost, snip off the roots and eat them raw, stir-fried or very quickly steamed or boiled.

MORE BASIL FOR YOUR MONEY

For many years I have grown basil from seed – starting it off either in a propagator or a warm greenhouse. It seems to be a slow process, though once it gets going by midsummer it will keep going and going until the first frosts. However, it is possible to get ahead with a supermarket plant, save time and money, involve little fear of failure and is another example of the wonder that is our natural world.

YOU WILL NEED
1 supermarket basil plant
scissors
small glass jars
sunny windowsill
7.5cm (3 inch) plant pots and peat-free compost (3 weeks later)

When you get your basil plant home, simply cut off the longest stems just below a leaf node. Remove the bottom leaves and any very large leaves and pop the stem into water.

Repeat with as many stems as you would like plants and leave them to root on a sunny windowsill.

Refresh the water every couple of days and in about 10 days you will see the first signs of tiny roots at the base. After 2 weeks, the roots will be about 2.5–5cm (1–2 inches) long and ready to plant into 7.5cm (3 inch) pots.

I repot the mother basil plant – it too will flourish following a haircut and a fresh supply of compost. Lots of basil for minimal cost.

Basil will keep producing as long as you keep harvesting. Regularly take out the growing tips and the plants will become bushy and gorgeous. See notes on preserving basil in mid-summer on page 146.

Try experimenting with other shop bought herbs and plants. I have rooted mint, rosemary, sage and, to my surprise, noted that a cut cosmos flower in a vase grew herself a set of roots! As a general rule cut just below a leaf node and who knows what might happen.

HERB AND GARLIC BUTTER

Herb and garlic butter is delightfully simple to make and a handy 'go to' for jacket potatoes, for stirring through pasta, mashing with potatoes, making your own garlic bread and using as a base when frying onions or other vegetables.

Makes 16 discs

YOU WILL NEED
scissors (optional)
vegetable knife
saucepan (optional)
tongs or slotted spoon (optional)
chopping board
bowl
hand whisk
mixing bowl
wooden spoon
cereal packet liner

3 tbsp finely chopped fresh chives, wild garlic, parsley, basil
    or sage
125g (4¼oz) softened salted butter
tsp ground black pepper
½ tsp mixed dried herbs
1 tsp powdered garlic or 2 crushed fresh cloves (or to taste)

If using chives, cut them very finely with scissors; chop parsley and sage finely with a knife, or if using wild garlic or basil, I blanch the leaves first to retain their vibrant colour and flavours, making the butter suitable for freezing. Chopped chives, sage and parsley will freeze well without blanching, whereas I find wild garlic and basil can discolour and turn grey/black if not blanched first. This quick scalding of the leaves, followed by a thorough cooling, stops enzyme actions which otherwise cause loss of flavour, colour and texture.

If you need to blanch the herbs, fill a sink with cold water and bring a pan of water to a fast boil, drop in the fresh leaves (no need to wash them first) and blanch for 1 minute. Quickly remove the wilted leaves with tongs or a slotted spoon and drop them into the cold water. (The vibrant green blanching water can be used again, to make a veggie stock or add to soups or stews.) Once the leaves have cooled, remove from the cold water and squeeze out as much water as possible then blot them with kitchen paper or a dry tea towel to remove any remaining moisture. Cut the blanched leaves into small pieces on the chopping board.

Whisk the butter until soft and creamy then add the black pepper, mixed herbs, garlic and chopped herbs. Stir well to combine with a wooden spoon then taste and adjust the flavour by adding more pepper, garlic or herbs to suit your own palate.

Open out the cereal packet liner so it's laid out in a single sheet on the worktop, with the longest side facing you. Transfer the butter onto it in a large lump then spread the butter out on the sheet. Roll the sheet from the long side closest to you, enclosing the butter until you've achieved a tight sausage. Twist the ends of the sheet, imagining you are forming a Christmas cracker. I find twisting the right side clockwise and the left side anticlockwise tightens the butter to a sausage about 20cm (8 inches) long. Once it feels completely firm fold the ends under and pop into the freezer for an hour or two or until completely hard.

Remove the parcel from the freezer, remove the plastic (which will peel away easily) cut into neat 1cm (½ inch)-thick discs. Transfer the discs into a reusable plastic freezer box and use as required. This butter will keep for up to 6 months in the freezer, but I reckon you will have used it in no time as it is delicious.

A PLANET-FRIENDLY APPROACH FOR SLUGS, SNAILS AND OTHER PESTS

Whether you are container gardening, or have a garden, allotment or a veggie plot, enjoy a regular and routine check-up of your crops, to make sure weeds are being kept at bay and that nature's intruders are not enjoying your fresh veg before you get the chance to. Warm, humid conditions are perfect for growing but are also perfect for weeds, slugs, snails and other plant-loving pests.

In the past, at the first sign of insects I used to turn to slug pellets, greenfly sprays, caterpillar killers and every chemical product I could get my hands on. Nowadays, I feel that if I wanted to grow my food in this way I may as well save my time and buy supermarket produce instead and instead my now planet-friendly self has adapted a 'live and let live' approach.

Slugs and snails love warm, damp conditions, so they will adore sitting around in the strawberry patch or at the base of a row of spinach, munching as required. However, so too do frogs and toads – they adore this shady damp area and will feast on the slugs and snails and not your precious veg. Deterrents rather than treatments are my planet-friendly preferred approach: a rough grit made from 6 washed, crushed eggshells mixed with just half a teaspoon of table salt will provide a border around your favourite plants and slugs and snails will not cross this line – they'll do a quick U-turn when they feel a nip on their toes.

Chemical insect sprays do not discriminate, so as well as getting rid of the pesky creatures that infest our roses, veggies and young leaf growth, we also harm the ones that are more beneficial to our aims – those insects well known to us that we can't be without and we love, such as ladybirds, honey bees and colourful butterflies. Ladybirds and blue tits rely on a good supply of greenfly and aphids throughout the summer months, meaning their food supply is killed off too.

||||||||||||||||||||||||||||||||||||||||||||||||||||||||||||||||||||||||||||||||||||||||||||||||||||||||||||||||

TIP: Rather than eliminating greenfly, whitefly and aphids with harsh chemical nasties, a spray bottle filled with just water and aimed at close range will power-hose a cluster of greenfly from your prize rose bush buds onto the ground. Blast at the first sign of pests and in the evening when the air is still.

||||||||||||||||||||||||||||||||||||||||||||||||||||||||||||||||||||||||||||||||||||||||||||||||||||||||||||||||

I have found the best approach is to co-exist with insects when it comes to growing veggies. I plant strategically, growing early cauliflowers and cabbages which will mature in early spring just before the cabbage white butterfly starts laying her eggs;

I grow early carrots sown in spring that are ready to eat in early summer and by doing this have managed to sidestep carrot fly which hasn't quite got up to speed, and I then sow a crop in late summer when carrot fly are less active. I really think this works and is a natural way to deter and avoid, rather than treat, pests.

Never Forget Nasturtiums

Nasturtiums grown from seed in pots in early-mid spring can now be planted outdoors and it's still not too late to sow.

I have a wonderful story about the benefits of planting these flowers. I created a brand-new blackcurrant bed (having lost my previous stocks to disease some years earlier). The six bushes, though young and small, were looking green leafed and gorgeous. On one of my regular patrols around the garden I noticed the new tender green shoots were curling up at the ends and on closer inspection I spotted greenfly. Spraying is very much a last resort, because with the best will in the world not only am I spraying the offending greenfly, I am also likely to cause harm to beneficial insects and pollinators. Instead, I sprayed them with a blast of cold water – knocking them to the ground, and planted six young nasturtium plants – one at the base of each of my bushes – at the same time. Fast forward a number of weeks and by late summer the nasturtiums had grown to provide a thick carpet over the fruit bed, thereby keeping it moist, the bright orange flowers had attracted black fly, the leaves had clusters of greenfly here and there, caterpillars were happily munching on the leaves and ladybirds had joined in the fun too. My black-currants were absolutely untouched!

COMPANION PLANTING

Companion planting is the description given to planting side by side in a way that is mutually beneficial because each plant, whether it be fruit, veggie or flower grows happily together and one helps the other along. I find this really exciting and once I got my head around it and understood the concept and how it works when planting, it seemed to make perfect sense to me.

The benefits are that pests and diseases are controlled or deterred, pollination is improved, and soil nutrients are shared, resulting in there being little or no reliance on bug or disease treatments having to be used. This is an area I am still learning about and I find it intriguing and thoroughly rewarding and realise once again that nature has all the answers – we just need to ask the questions.

A row of onions, garlic or leeks alongside carrots, for example, is mutually beneficial. The strong scent of the leeks, onions and garlic repel carrot fly and carrots apparently repel leek moths. I have found it to be true about the carrot fly, though I have not suffered leek moths – maybe that is why!

When planting, therefore, be mindful and mix crops around, consider when pests are most prominent and avoid harvest times that fall around the times when bugs are busy (I tend choose early or late varieties of crops) and be mindful too that there are many veggies that are not that well favoured by bugs. Kale, for example, may attract a few aphids later on that seem to just like sitting around the leaves, not chewing or damaging them in any way. Spinach beet always does well for me too, in terms of pest resistance, as do leeks, runner and French beans.

My favourites are crops that are obviously nutritious, versatile and can be used in many ways, are long-lasting and will sit in the ground happily until I am ready to harvest, they do not necessarily need lots of space or care, they are not that attractive to pests and most of all are easy to grow.

EASY CROPS:
Broad beans, French beans, runner beans, peas, kale, spinach, onions, leeks, parsnips, early carrots and cauliflowers, salads, tomatoes, aubergines, courgettes, sweetcorn, raspberries, strawberries, early potatoes, spring cabbage, beetroot, turnips, rhubarb, sprouts.

I am enjoying embracing the idea that crops can be 'mates' in the garden and if you grow potatoes then try planting a row of something from the cabbage family alongside. Cabbages and cauliflowers have shallow root systems so won't be competing for the potatoes' nutrients. Beetroots are good mates with cabbages too. Also beans and peas planted alongside potatoes will help them to thrive because they release nitrogen back into the soil. I will revisit this wonder of nature in midsummer when we can see evidence of 'natural' fertiliser for ourselves (see page 140).

Growing in a limited space at home or in pots means we can enjoy a diverse range of mutually beneficial crops and grow a variety just as nature intended.

Similarly, I found out to my cost that planting crops of the same type side by side is not always a good idea. One year I decided to have a 'root' bed. I considered this to be fantastic plan – after all, we see fields full of the same crop. I quite fancied the idea of a bed full of my favourite root veggies. I found out to my cost that only the carrots and beetroot did well because they matured first. The remainder – the parsnips, turnips, celeriac and swede – ended up producing feeble, small, though still edible veg.

Disappointed at the result of what I thought was a genius plan, I realised that what I had actually done was create huge competition for the same set of nutrients. All the root crops needed the same foods, so the early croppers took it all, leaving the slower-growing, later-maturing veggies to be starved.

When we see fields full of the same crops it is now so very obvious to me that they have to rely on more than the natural nutrients in the soil. Non-organic farming methods involve the addition of chemical fertilisers, treatments, sprays, pesticides and insecticides in order to provide us with large volumes of perfect-looking produce. Even more of a reason, if you have some space, to grow your own and know that everything about it is natural.

Gardening and growing is like most other things – the more you know, the more there is to know. I had read about rotating crops, i.e., not growing the same plant in the same place year after year, because this can attract problems of disease and result in a failure to thrive, but I have since learned that while this may be essential for farmers, for the home grower it is not necessary. When I considered my own veggie space, I realised that my rhubarb grows in the same spot year after year, as do my fruit bushes, so surely as long as my soil is healthy and nutritious I don't need to get so hung up about crop rotation, the fear of disease and the worry about planting the same thing in the same place every year.

What is important is the need to keep the ground healthy and nutritious, and the organic way to do this is to simply add lots of good compost in the autumn. I am completely hooked now on 'no dig' gardening techniques, which it is suggested may go back as far as pre-industrial or 19th century farming methods. I love to read around the reason for things and would love to have met the Japanese farmer and philosopher Masanobu Fukuoka – this 'do nothing' farmer was celebrated for his natural farming and re-vegetation of deserted lands. He was an outspoken advocate of the value of observing nature's principles. This makes so much sense to me now, though am no expert by any means but – just like humans – any living thing in the natural world if healthy will resist pests and disease.

I am really 'on it' now when planning my planting. Whereas in the past I would sprinkle a row of seeds or dig in a few small cabbages or beans just where there was a space or where it took my fancy, I now take a few minutes to consider which plants like each other and try to encourage a lasting friendship by planting them side by side. Here are a few examples of the ways I mix my planting:

- Rhubarb repels insects so I plant my cabbages and sprouts next door so that the butterflies will find some other leaves on which to lay their eggs.
- Onions, leeks and garlic give off an insect-repelling scent, so I plant carrots alongside and the alliums deter the carrot fly.
- Crops such as parsnips, swede, potatoes and turnips will flourish and enjoy being neighbours with beans and peas. Peas and beans are collectively referred to as legumes and they store excess nitrogen in their roots which is just the job for a crop that is maturing below ground.
- The site of a crop of peas and beans, once finished, can be planted afterwards with courgettes which will feast heartily on the nitrogen left in the soil. High levels of nitrogen promote lots of foliage growth, which is perfect too for cabbages, sprouts, cauliflowers and of course kale. When my peas and beans finish in goes my kale which will feed me right through the winter months.
- Runner beans and sweetcorn are great partners and I have read that corn, beans and squash grow incredibly well together. I have planted sweetcorn and beans side by side: the scarlet flowers on runner beans come just at the right time to attract bees and other insects, which help to pollinate the equally tall sweetcorn. The runner beans release nitrogen into the soil which helps sustain the hungry corn and they provide each other with much welcome shade on the very hot days. Both of these tall-growing crops leave lots of space on the ground beneath them so in go any spare courgette plants as ground cover.

This can all be very confusing, so I give myself three general rules:

1. Avoid planting too many crops of the same type together (like my root bed).
2. A root crop (e.g., parsnip, potato) very often likes living next door to legumes (e.g., beans, peas).
3. Insect-attracting brassicas (e.g., cabbages and cauliflowers) thrive better next to alliums (e.g., onions, shallots and garlic) as their pungent smell is perfect for repelling pests. For readers with small gardens and for those growing food in pots that may not have the room or desire for onion growing, adding a few marigolds (or dare I say again – nasturtiums) here and there will provide a deterrent 'smoke screen' as insects love them. They are an edible plant, though I grow them more for their colour and companion planting benefits.

SUMMER

EARLY SUMMER

I n Britain, June is often referred to as 'Flaming June' (also the name of a popular Victorian painting by Sir Frederic Leighton, 1895) but, for many, the weather is rarely flaming and is generally unsettled. When the sun does shine, it is HOT. Pair that with regular downpours of rain and we have a perfect growing climate.

Veggies and fruit seem to grow almost before your very eyes. The first strawberries are here, and I think it has to be said that nothing compares to a fresh British strawberry. Strawberries grow very well in pots and hanging baskets but the birds love them too. The netted frame that I place over my strawberry bed once I see the first sign of fruits ensures that I get to enjoy them!

By early summer I harvest my first raspberries, and the very first root of my finest new potatoes. Enjoy the rapid growth that early summer brings and harvest your very young, tender crops regularly. The summer solstice promises we can enjoy around sixteen hours of daylight which is also, of course, sixteen hours of growing and gardening time.

Cut Sweet Peas

Early summer promises to supply your very first bunch of fragrant colourful sweet peas and what starts off as half a dozen stems in a small vase will soon be filling several vases every week. It is important to cut sweet peas regularly. The more the flowers are picked, the more will be produced. Make sure your sweet pea plants don't dry out, cut off any tiny green pods that you see forming with scissors – if they form seed pods the plant will cease to produce flowers – cut the blooms at least once a week, fill your home with their delicate, distinct perfume and colour and enjoy every minute.

During this wonderful season I tend to pick all of my blooms one day a week and fill the house with their perfume, and usually have a cleaning session the same day. The house is clean and sparkling, and the sweet peas provide a final fresh, beautiful, natural room refresher. I cut every single flower and bud from my sweet peas to keep them going.

Behead Broad Beans

Broad beans will be growing tall and the tightly packed cluster of leaves at the top of the plant will often attract blackfly. The clusters of tiny black flies appear immobile and you will probably spy a few ants hanging around too. I used to think the ants were munching on the blackfly until I discovered they are actually the best of friends. Blackfly secrete a sugary substance which ants love – you will notice this substance because the leaves become sticky. In order to protect their food supply, the ants will look after the blackfly, until the ladybirds and small wild birds move in and munch any blackfly or aphids, refusing to be deterred by the ants! The vigilant grower will be in attendance well before blackfly and ants become a nuisance, and they can be sorted in a few minutes at the right time without the need for harmful pesticides.

Inspect your broad beans regularly and you'll notice your plants will be showing signs of their first pods. Tiny and only about 2.5cm (1 inch) long, they form after the fragrant black and white flowers have faded and these are the very beginnings of your crop. Once you have counted three sets of pods, however small, then you can stop blackfly in their tracks. The first pods will be at the bottom of the plant, about 20cm (8 inches) from the ground, then follow the stem upwards and in another 15cm (6 inches) you will see another pod and then 15cm (6 inches) higher a third. That is perfect – the plant needs to produce three sets of pods. Take your thumb and forefinger and nip out the growing tips of your broad bean plants, blackfly and all!

By nipping out the tender growing tip (just as we did with sweet peas in early spring – see page 42) the plants are encouraged to concentrate energy not on growing upwards any longer but outwards, and into fattening and filling the pods. A broad bean plant that is left to grow only upwards will not yield as many beans.

The discarded tips can be tossed onto the compost bin. Even if your plants don't suffer blackfly (though I have yet to enjoy a year without them), still reduce the growing height of your broad beans in this way. The same applies to taller-growing runner beans and French beans. Once the plant reaches the top of the canes, nip out the growing tip to encourage bushier growth and flowers lower down bearing more beans that you can actually reach.

Pepper, Chilli and Aubergine Plants

Seeds sown in early spring in a propagator, or later directly into pots, will be small bushy plants and growing bigger by the day. Look out for flower buds – a sure sign that their fabulous fruits will follow.

The Luffa Gourd Challenge

My first attempt – no germination. Two years later and a second attempt – lots of green growth but no flowers. My third attempt and this season I found flowers! Bright yellow gorgeous flowers growing with a tiny luffa behind. Fingers crossed that this might be *the* year!

Plant Sweetcorn

Early crops of potatoes, salads, onions, shallots and garlic, once harvested, will create extra space, and after a quick weed of the areas and rake over, any pots of sweetcorn waiting in the wings can now be planted in the ground. Rather than planting sweetcorn in distinct rows, the recommendation is to plant them in a square bed to help with pollination. For example, if you have 16 plants, rather than setting them in a single row 46cm (18 inches) apart, plant them in a square area 4 plants x 4 plants and still 46cm (18 inches) apart.

As mentioned on page 118, sweetcorn is a great companion for runner beans so, when planning your bed, think about planting these tall crops side by side. You could plant your sweetcorn in a square bed and train your runner beans up a pyramid construction alongside.

If you have spare courgette plants, pop them in at the feet of the sweetcorn. The tall sweetcorn will enjoy having their heads in the fresh air, the courgettes will be more than happy to hug the ground.

Courgettes

Any courgettes that have been growing patiently in pots can now be given freedom of movement and transferred to their permanent bed once autumn-planted onions, garlic, shallots and early potatoes have been harvested.

Get Ready for Raspberries

The tight clusters of buds followed by tiny white flowers that appeared last season will now be small green berries forming on summer-fruiting raspberry canes. By the end of the season the berries will fatten, turn a pale pink, then almost overnight will transform to plump red berries. I have grown raspberries for many years and, other than the first few fruits, the birds tend to leave them alone, probably because there is an abundance of alternative, easier to harvest, fresh produce at this time. I have not had the need to protect my raspberries from birds. The low-hanging fruits, on the other hand, used to be a favourite of my old dog Charlie. He knew when it was raspberry time and would join me fruit picking. Mine went into a bowl, his straight into his mouth!

Check in on Potatoes

Early potatoes planted back in early spring (see page 50) will now be huge bushy plants and at last you will notice the first of the flowers. These often pale lilac or white flowers are **not** edible even though they are quite pretty. A good show of flowers is, however, a reliable indicator that the potatoes are maturing and that they are worth a look.

I find this so nostalgic – I have a memory of helping my grandad as a very small child. He used to say, 'Shall we get a root?' and I thought it the most exciting thing of all. He had a potato fork which had thick prongs with rounded ends so that the potatoes didn't get stabbed or cut when lifting. He used to unearth the potatoes and I used to be on my knees, face to the ground, ready to see. He would say 'Are there any? I can't see from here.' I used to scream with delight, 'Grandad, there are hundreds!' Every year without fail this memory comes flooding back as I unearth my first root of potatoes.

For the first root I start at the end of the row. I check first with a hand trowel, just gently teasing the soil away and digging down. You will see in an instant whether your potatoes are plump enough for harvesting and, if they are no bigger than pebble size, gently cover them up again and come back in a week or so. My first root is always harvested when too small as I am so impatient, and it is my guess that you'll go for it then too.

The very thin papery skins will simply rub off and they can go straight into the pan or steamer – there is nothing that compares: the shops can never deliver this degree of freshness and the corresponding superior taste. 'Fast food' has a very different meaning in this context.

SEASONAL SPECIAL – ELDERFLOWER SYRUP

While there's lots of activity in the garden, it is also a great time for foraging, with the hedgerows offering delicious free pickings. Elder trees that seem fairly nondescript at other times of the year have a short flowering season from late spring to early summer, with beautiful pale off-white to cream tiny star-shaped fragrant and edible clusters of blooms. I always think they resemble a massive show of sun parasols, looking as though they're made from the finest lace and offering welcome cool shade from the early strong summer sunshine to the dark green elder leaves sitting below. Elderflowers are one of my favourite edibles to forage – though the pale pink wild rose in flower at this time may edge them into second place. I once went through a phase of making wild rose ice cream!

Elderflowers eaten on their own leave a bitter aftertaste, but this syrup is something else! When you capture the delicate unique elderflower perfume and pair it with lemons and sugar, it is little wonder it became a royal wedding cake flavour choice.

Lemon and elderflower also team up perfectly with tart fruits such as gooseberries and rhubarb which are also now ready to harvest. Pairing elderflower with these flavours makes for an absolutely unique, stunning summer flavour profile. Mother Nature has it all there in her basket. What grows together often goes together – we just have to do the picking.

This syrup makes the perfect flavour addition for a butter-cream or jelly, or to sweeten gooseberries and rhubarb rather than using sugar on its own. I also add it to fruit salads and ice creams, stir it into cream when making a pavlova or simply dilute it with fizzy water to make a refreshing non-alcoholic drink.

Makes 3 litres (about 5 pints)

YOU WILL NEED
mesh bag for foraging the flowers
scissors
large saucepan
grater, potato peeler, speed peeler or zester for the lemons
vegetable knife
fine muslin or jelly bag
colander
large preserving pan with a lid and your largest saucepan
plastic or sterilised glass bottles

500g (1lb 2oz) elderflower heads yielding 370g (13oz) flowers
2kg (4lb 8oz) granulated sugar
1.5 litres (50fl oz) cold water
60g (2¼oz) citric acid
2 large unwaxed lemons

I collect my flowers in a fine mesh bag that holds onto the flowers but allows bugs or flies in the flowers to shake out while I am still foraging or walking home. Look for fresh, bright flowers and avoid any that are brown and beginning to fade. Cut from the tree with scissors and choose those that are at eye level or just above so that dogs have not been near when looking for a toilet spot. I do not wash the blooms, just give them a gentle tap so that any hidden bugs drop out.

Once home, use your flowers straight away. Cut the thick green stalks from the blooms (the handles of the parasol), then weigh your trimmed harvest and adjust the other ingredients accordingly. So, for example, if after trimming my foraged bag of blooms, the remaining flowers weigh 200g (7oz). Looking to the ingredients opposite, I would need to halve the remaining ingredients to make 1.5 litres (2½ pints) of syrup.

Place the sugar in the large saucepan, pour over the water and stir over a low heat until the sugar dissolves and the water is clear. Add the citric acid (which will help preserve the syrup) and stir until this too dissolves. Pare the zest from the lemons and add to the syrup, then slice the zested fruits thinly and add them to the pan. Add the flower heads, stir and bring to the boil, then turn off the heat, give a final stir, cover the pan and transfer to a cool place and leave for 24 hours.

The next day, strain the syrup through a fine piece of muslin or jelly bag secured over a colander hooked over the second saucepan. Boil the syrup once more, then turn off the heat. Either bottle it straight away in sterilised bottles (see page 68) or leave the syrup to cool and pour into plastic bottles to be kept in the fridge for up to 6 weeks, or freeze for a year. If freezing, allow some room for the liquid to expand. Once chilled, the syrup may look cloudy but just give it a shake and it will clear.

TIP: Try making a crumble and drizzling over 1–2 tablespoons of the syrup over the fruit to sweeten it (instead of sugar) before adding the topping – the flavour is absolutely unbelievable.

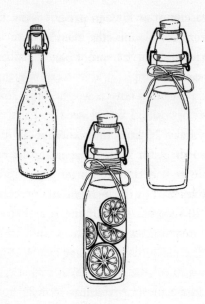

STORING HERBS – STALKS AND ALL!

Even in a small or limited growing space, from early summer onwards it is still possible to grow more than you can eat. Surplus stocks of fresh herbs are delicious and can be dried or frozen for winter use. The huge leaves from a flourishing pot of parsley, for example, preserve well. To harvest them, don't be tempted to remove just the leaves – cut right down to the base of the plant and remove the stalk too.

TO FREEZE

Remove the stalks from the leaves and freeze these separately in a bag or box – they are a great addition when making stock. Tear the leaves into smaller pieces then blitz to a large crumb in a food processor fitted with the blade attachment. Line a tray with greaseproof or kitchen paper, scatter the leaves over and open-freeze for 30 minutes, then tip the frozen crumbs from the paper into a freezer-proof box to seal and use during the winter months.

TO DRY

I have a dehydrator but this microwave method works just as well. Take two sheets of kitchen paper and lay one sheet on a microwaveable tray or plate. Scatter over a single layer of chopped herb leaves. Lay the second piece over then microwave on high for 20 seconds. Lift off the top sheet of paper. The leaves will be steaming so fluff them around, lay over the paper again and this time turn the wattage down to just 100 watts and microwave for a further 20 minutes. Check halfway through, but I have found 20 minutes to be just about sufficient time to completely dry the herbs.

Once completely cool, use the bottom sheet of paper to funnel your dried herbs into clean, old herb or spice storage jars.

HARVESTING, DRYING AND STORING AUTUMN-PLANTED ONIONS, SHALLOTS AND GARLIC

Over the past few years I have favoured autumn sowings as an alternative to spring. Autumn-sown crops are ready in early summer, rather than autumn, thereby freeing valuable growing space for another crop that will be ready to harvest in late summer. I have sweetcorn eagerly waiting in pots ready to jump into the bed once the onions and other early summer veg have been harvested.

The tops of autumn-sown varieties will begin to flop over in early summer. The thick smooth stems which were tall, strong and vivid green will fade in colour, some will seem to be withering and dying and then they will fall flat onto the ground. Don't be alarmed – this is simply the sign that the onion bulb below has stopped growing and it will soon be time to harvest.

The whole bed can look quite unwieldy with dead, dying and some still green leaves laying this way and that so I like to tidy the row up a bit, gathering the splayed leaves in one hand and laying them neatly in one direction so that the bulbs look like heads and the leaves, some dried and some green resemble grass skirts below. Left in this state for a week or so to lap up more sunshine will complete the drying process.

Whenever onions, garlic and shallots are planted, the method for harvesting and storage is exactly the same. Spring-planted varieties are ready to harvest in late summer, but for those planted the previous autumn, they will be ready any time now.

To do this I choose a dry day and, rather than pull at the dried top (which may result in the top and bulb coming apart), I take a small hand fork or trowel just to help lift the onion bulb complete with roots. Gently rub off any soil from the underside of the bulb and roots then take the whole onion, garlic bulb or shallot and transfer to a bright, sunny and dry place for a few days to finish drying out.

I have netting frames that I use to cover seedlings at the start of the year and, when out of use, they are stored by the compost area. I find this a perfect place to dry my onions, because the air can circulate all around them, but a slatted garden seat or table is also fine. If a rainy spell is forecast, take the onions into a cool, dry place to finish drying.

Onions, garlic and shallots when dried well, can be stored for up to six months and sometimes even longer - though check the variety is recommended for storing when choosing seeds or sets (bulbs). Once dry, the trimmed onions can be stored in netting bags, but I favour stringing them. I love to see strings of onions ready for winter use. Garlic and shallots can be braided and when done well can look almost too good to eat. If you don't have the time or inclination for stringing, try popping onions into the leg of an old pair of tights, with a knot between each one, which can then be hung up and cut off as required.

Only use well-dried onions for stringing or storing. Set aside any with a soft spot or any that don't look absolutely perfect, cut off any imperfect bits, then use them up rather than store or simply chop up and freeze if there are too many to use at once.

Trim the dried-up roots with scissors: holding the onion in one hand, make a fist around the dried stalk and with the other hand cut about 2.5cm (1 inch) above, leaving about 13cm (5 inch) of dried stalk remaining.

Take a length of string about 1 metre (3 ft, 3 inches) and tie the two ends together (I loop the string around my fence post with the knot of the string at the top). Make an upward-facing loop at the other end of the string, take the first onion, pop the stalk into the loop, pull the onion downwards and the string will tighten itself around the neck of the first onion. Pull tightly to secure.

Weave the dried stalk upwards between the two taut lengths of string. Take the second onion and this time, rather than weave the stalk upwards, slot the onion between the two lengths of string with the stalk facing downwards and then weave it between the two lengths.

Continue with more onions, slotting the onion between the strings facing downwards and weaving the dried leaves below. I find 8–10 onions on a string is sufficient, otherwise the strings get too heavy.

Garlic can be strung in the same way, but for shallots I simply store them in netted onion bags. Alternatively, again, an upcycled pair of old tights can be used and simply pop in separate legs your onions, garlic and shallots!

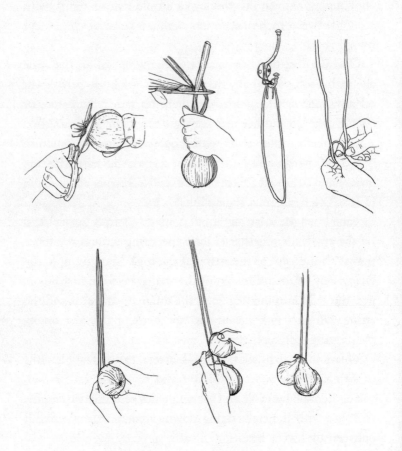

MIDSUMMER

In summertime the garden is gorgeous and the sun is shining, but what do you do about your precious fruit and veggies if you want to go away on holiday for a week or two? I spend considerable time looking after my crops every day – watering, weeding, pinching out the side shoots from my tomatoes and generally pottering about – and worry when it comes to leaving them. How many times have you been away on holiday only to then come back and . . . oh my goodness, I am convinced the garden grows quicker when we go away!

If you have a good neighbour or friend, then the watering and general care can be managed in your absence, and the offer of free fruit and veggies is always welcomed by the garden caretaker or babysitter.

If you have a greenhouse, it is essential in warm weather that the windows can open allowing cooler air to circulate. In very hot weather, I dampen down the greenhouse: as well as watering and spraying the plants, I water the floor too, which creates a humid rather than dry environment for the growing plants. If you are going away, leave full cans of water in your greenhouse so that your friendly caretaker can quickly and easily do this for you.

You know how I like to throw in an experiential story here and there – well, here is a good one. Before going on holiday one year, I had a beautiful healthy row of spinach beet. I thoroughly recommend it by the way: the lush green leaves are packed with vitamins and very tasty in stir fries, vegetable lasagne and soups; it doesn't attract pests; for the gardener with not much space it is perfect because the same plant will continue to produce young tender tasty leaves over and over again; and in the growing season it produces leaves as fast as you can eat them (remove the outside leaves first and work inwards). However, it can quickly bolt and go to seed, and this can often happen if it gets stressed through lack of water or because of a cold snap. From the centre of the plant a thickened stalk will appear which will then produce buds for flowers. All of the energy is diverted to this one stalk, the outside leaves begin to look frail and limp and, once this has happened, the advice is to dig it up and discard it because there is no going back once bolted.

I remember my disappointment to see, when I returned from a two-week holiday, that just about each and every spinach beet plant in my row had produced the aforementioned thick-ened stem and flower buds. I got out my garden fork and began to uplift my fallen spinach, but then thought hang on a minute, I can feel an experiment coming on! I left half of the row in the ground and, instead of digging it out, gave it a thorough, brutal haircut, cutting every leaf and stem down to within 2.5–5cm (1–2 inches) of ground level and giving them a good watering. I then left them. I had absolutely nothing to lose and maybe something to gain. You have prob-ably guessed what happened – within a few days, I spotted tiny fresh new green leaves reaching upwards for the light and within a week or so they were flapping around gloriously in the summer breeze and I was happily harvesting once more. Then, and with no exaggeration, this half row of spinach continued to produce leaves, with no further bolting, stalks or flowers, right through until the following March keeping me in fresh greens right through the winter. It survived several frosts and a light fall of snow. The moral of the story – don't be afraid to break the rules and if something gives you that gut feeling – give it a go because my experience is that plants really do want to grow and will do their very best for you.

Veggies, salads and herbs grown in pots will now be filling your growing area, looking colourful, vibrant and very productive. Courgettes will be providing an almost daily supply, tomatoes will be ripening, and for the new keen grower this is a very exciting time. Even though there may have been a heavy downpour of rain, which is hugely helpful and beneficial to veggies growing in beds, it is still important to head over to your supply of rain water (from the biggest water butt you have room for) to water pots, containers and hanging baskets daily, even twice daily on very hot or very windy days.

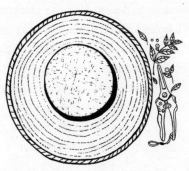

Harvest Peas and Beans

To harvest peas and beans, be mindful to pull downwards on the pod. This is particularly important for broad beans: the pods can be large and pulling one upwards can result in the whole plant being lifted from the ground. I hold onto the main stem with one hand and gently hold onto the pod with my other hand, then twist where the pod fixes to the stem and at the same time pull downwards. The pod then leaves the stem cleanly without dislodging the rest of the plant. The lower pods will ripen first. Broad beans are ready to harvest when the pods are about 15–20cm (6–8 inches) long and when squeezed they should feel firm and full inside. Peas are ready when they are about 10cm (4 inches) in length, and are swollen with the peas inside. Again, gently twist and pull them downwards to remove them from the plant.

Your early-sown peas and broad beans may well have finished cropping by now, their harvest having been enjoyed fresh on the plate, with any surplus frozen for the winter.

Once you've harvested all your peas and beans, take a few minutes to marvel at another wonder of nature: lift one root from your spent row of peas or beans – only one because all of the others will be left in the ground – and inspect the bunch of small roots. You'll see a number of tiny grey clusters fixed here and there. These rough-looking grey balls or 'nodules' are tiny sacks of nature's own nitrogen fertiliser, which the plant is storing because it has found it is surplus to requirements. How fantastic is that!

So that the next crop going in can enjoy this energy boost, take a pair of scissors or secateurs and cut the pea and bean stems (French beans, runner beans, broad beans, peas and mangetout) off at ground level. The stems can go into the compost bin, but the roots with their sacks of natural fertiliser will stay below ground ready to feed the next plantings.

See Companion Planting on page 114 to ensure your crops will get maximum benefit from their planting position. A row of kale or spring cabbage plants will thoroughly enjoy being planted after beans.

Pinch Out Side Shoots on Tomatoes

Continue to pinch out the side shoots from your tomato plants – you want all energy to be used by the plant to fatten up the tomatoes, not grow extra leaves. This was one of the first-ever gardening jobs given to me as a child. I had to check them every day – they don't grow that quickly by the way, I think it was just that I wasn't too vigilant back in the day and used to miss a few.

The side shoots can be simply added to the compost bin or popped into water. In around two weeks these side shoots will have grown roots and can be planted into small pots and grown on and thereby keep your tomato plant supply going for longer. See over the page for illustration. At the time of writing I have a number of small plants that I am hoping to over-winter indoors so that I have a head start next spring. Finger crossed.

This season will also produce your first ripe tomato and what a joy it is. I am always puzzled as to why one single tomato from a cluster of many on a vine should be the first to go bright red, when its sisters sitting either side are still green, but again that is a wonder of nature. Whatever the

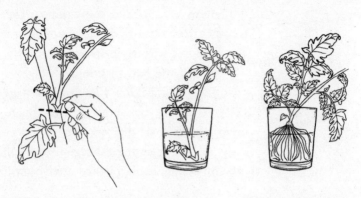

reason, I carefully remove it and enjoy it there and then while it's still warm – priceless. There are so many tomato varieties to choose from – many ripening to red, some to yellow, some variegated whilst other varieties remain green but are sweet and delicious.

Another 5-minute job: remove some of the bottom leaves from your tomato plants with a pair of large scissors or secateurs to allow air to circulate and the sun to get to the low-hanging fruits.

By the way, if your tomatoes split on the vine it is usually because their water supply has been inconsistent so be sure to keep them well irrigated as the tomatoes fatten up and remember to continue with a weekly plant feed (see page 180) or buy an organic tomato feed especially if your tomatoes are growing in bags or pots where they will soon use up the nutrients that are contained in the compost material.

Take a Snap of Your Sweet Peas

Your sweet peas will be looking resplendent. It's a good idea to take a photo of your plants – if it is your plan to collect the seeds in autumn (see page 189) because by then the plants may well have faded so much so that the original flashes of colour may be long gone, so taking photos will help you recall the colours.

I had a deep red sweet-pea flower that was so beautiful but did not take a photo as an aide memoire. I fear I may not have known which plant it came from but it didn't matter hugely as I still enjoyed them mixed along with the others.

Enjoy Raspberries

Towards the end of this season, the summer fruiting raspberries will be few and far between. They are wonderful though – how fantastic to be picking fresh berries for six whole weeks! You will be notice new bright-green growth coming from the base of the plants. Don't be tempted to pull these out because what you have going on here is the beginnings of next year's fruiting canes. By the end of the summer, they will be tall, big and strong!

Thin Out Apples for a Stronger Crop

Around this time you may notice small cherry-tomato-sized baby apples lying around on the ground – this is often referred to as the 'July drop'. This is nothing to worry about, it's just nature's way of discarding the weakling fruits to make room for the stronger ones. I often help things along with a pair of scissors at this time too, reducing a large cluster of 4 or 5 small apples by 1 or 2, clipping off the smallest. It does make a difference because rather than 4 or 5 small-sized fruits in the autumn I can look forward to 2 or 3 bumper-sized apples. Any weakling fruits, often too small, dry and bitter to eat, can be added to the compost.

Stop Harvesting Rhubarb

Rhubarb will still be looking happy, though the stalks may be thickening and beginning to colour green rather than red. My crowns have kept me supplied since late winter and, even though they are still eager to please, now is the time to stop harvesting if it is to be as gorgeous next year. There's no need to do anything to it other than leave it alone – consider this season finished. I always remind myself that it has served me well and is now stepping aside to allow me to look forward to the fruits from the months that will follow.

The Luffa Gourd Challenge

By midsummer the baby luffas had dropped off, yet the plant is huge and healthy with lots of leaves – it reaches the very top of the greenhouse. I then discover clusters of yellow flowers, not single ones as before bearing a baby luffa. These are clusters of male flowers, yet the timing seems to be all wrong – the female flowers have since faded and dropped off by the time the blokes arrive! I do some online research to discover that hand pollination may have been necessary… this really is a challenge! Have I missed my opportunity? I had the female flowers but not a male in sight. Now lots of males and not a girl to be seen.

Beetroot

The row of seedlings that were thinned out to 10cm (4 inches) apart back in spring (page 82) will now be an imposing row of large and tall red/green bushy leaves and, when these are lifted, a row of gorgeous beetroots will be revealed. I am usually impatient to taste this amazing vegetable, so I start by harvesting a few golf-ball-sized roots, leaving the larger ones to grow that bit longer. I will carry out the main harvest in late summer. I will pickle a few in jars, but the majority will be stored fresh and whole for winter use.

Curing Potatoes

When I had less growing space, I used to grow only a few potatoes to enjoy fresh but now I grow more so that I can store them for later in the year. I leave some of my potatoes in the ground until midsummer, by which time the tops have died down and are lying yellow, dried and limp on the ground. I harvest the potatoes which are now much larger. To cure them (making them suitable for storage), I place them in a cool dark place with good air circulation so that the skins can thicken and firm up.

To do this, harvest when the weather is dry then rub off any soil with your hands and lay them in a single layer. I use my apple store (the perfect out-of-season use for the bit of kit) though you can lay them on wooden racks or shelves in a shed or garage. There they will stay for two weeks. After this time the skins have dried and feel thicker and I can then store them in paper sacks for later use.

STORING BASIL

Basil is in its element at this time. It loves the heat and sunshine and will grow quickly. Remember to harvest regularly, taking out growing tips and large leaves – this will keep your plants compact, bushy and they will not form flowers. The flowers are edible, by the way, but some can taste bitter so I tend to nip them out.

Basil is probably my favourite herb – its unique fresh fragrance and vibrant colour are so nostalgic. I had never tasted basil or rocket until I went on holiday to Italy in my thirties and every time I smell it the memories of that holiday, along with the sunshine, comes flooding back. Oh my word – what a revelation it was! I think if it wasn't for herbs and spices, food would be a fairly bland affair.

When it comes to storing and preserving basil for use during the winter, I have been disappointed that the fresh pungent flavour and aroma is often somewhat lacking: dried basil lacks that special pungency (though is still handy to have in the cupboard) and freezing it raw doesn't work because the leaves turn black. Blanching the leaves, making a pesto, then freezing it in ice cube trays is always a favourite, but if you want a quick, easy and successful preserving method then try making this paste. Unlike pesto, it is not very oily.

Basil and Fresh Herb Pots

Freezing fresh basil and any garden herbs in oil preserves the green colour and unique flavour and is a great 'go to' during the winter months when fresh basil and small packets of fresh herbs are expensive in the shops. A cube removed from the freezer thaws in 5-10 minutes and is ready to use adding a welcome layer of summer-fresh flavour to winter foods: add to soups, salads, dressings, pasta – any recipe that calls for fresh basil or herbs. I like to add a small cube over freshly cooked carrots, to a bowl of tomato soup, and to a steaming hot cheese-topped jacket potato

Makes 12 herb pots

YOU WILL NEED
food processor
12 hole silicone moulded tray (I have a small tray that I think
    is for chocolate moulds but is perfect for this)
teaspoon
freezer-proof box for storage

80g (2¾oz) fresh basil leaves (without stalks)
    or for fresh herb pots I like to use a mix of thyme,
        rosemary, mint, parsley (again without stalks)
1 tbsp rapeseed or olive oil

As my basil and herbs are home grown (I don't use sprays and the basil is grown under glass) I don't wash the leaves. If you need to wash your basil or herbs, make certain leaves are completely dry and have been trimmed of stalks before you begin.

Place the leaves in a food processor and blitz for a few seconds: the leaves will have reduced to a thin layer at the base. Keep the motor running and add the oil – it is a very small amount, just enough to coat the leaves and protect them in the freezer.

Spoon the coarse paste into the silicone tray and push it down with the back of the spoon. Freeze for several hours or until hard, then pop out of the silicone tray and store in a freezer-proof box to use as required.

RUNNER BEANS

The Victorians used to grow runner beans as much for their flower display as for the beans, and the bees love them too, so it is no wonder that a pyramid of runner beans does not look out of place in the flower garden. As the clusters of scarlet flowers fade, tiny slim tender pods will follow and timing wise, in my garden, these will mature slightly later than peas and broad beans.

Eat the pods whole when they are young and before they have developed a tough 'string' down the pod. The perfect size is 15–20cm (6–8 inches) long, when the pods are dark green and slim (not bulging with fat beans inside). The pod should easily snap in two when bent.

As the beans grow the pods thicken, toughen and turn from a dark green to a paler green. I believe so many people who say they don't like runner beans have eaten them when they have been allowed to get to this 'over-grown' state.

I have a vintage Spong bean slicer – I would like to boast that it's a family heirloom but it's not, I bought it off eBay about ten years ago now – a purpose-made tool dating back to the beginning of the 20th century, which has a hole for the bean that's just the right size. If the bean is too big (and therefore not as tender) the bean will not fit in the hole. Genius.

My runner-bean crops are usually huge, the freezer will be filling up and I find freezing runner beans – unlike French or broad beans – quite tedious. They are not an easy crop to blanch without overcooking, and they hold on to water, resulting in clumps of frozen beans. I was about ten when my grandad bought our first domestic freezer. Up until then, and for some years afterwards (my grandmother didn't trust the freezer), our runner beans used to be preserved in a delicious pickle.

Pickled Runner Beans

I urge you to try this pickle – it's absolutely delicious. As well as serving it with cheese and pies I like to add a tablespoon or two of the pickled beans to stews, soups and casseroles to give them an extra layer of flavour.

YOU WILL NEED
6 x 450g (1lb) clean glass jam jars with screw-top lids
large saucepan or casserole with a lid
medium saucepan
colander
small bowl

900ml (30fl oz) distilled white vinegar
800g (1lb 12oz) onions, thinly sliced

1kg (2lb 4oz) runner beans, trimmed and thinly sliced

1 tbsp curry powder

1 tbsp ground turmeric

1 tbsp English mustard powder

50g (1¾oz) cornflour

2 tbsp mustard seeds

600g (1lb 5oz) granulated or demerara sugar

3 red chillies, thinly sliced

Wash the glass jars and lids, making sure the lids are free from any rust or corrosion. To sterilise your jars before use, place them in a cold oven, heat to 100°C (Gas Mark ¼, 210°F) – leave them for half an hour then turn off the heat and leave the jars inside until ready to use.

Pour 300ml (10fl oz) of the vinegar into the large pan and add the onions. Bring to the boil, then reduce the heat, cover and simmer for 15 minutes.

Half fill the other saucepan with water, bring to the boil, drop in the beans and cook them for 5 minutes then strain in a colander.

Put the curry powder, turmeric, mustard powder and cornflour in a small bowl with a few tablespoons of the remaining vinegar and mix to form a smooth paste. Stir in the mustard seeds.

Add the remaining vinegar and the sugar to the pan containing the onions, increase the heat and stir until the sugar has dissolved. Add the paste and stir, then add the beans and sliced chillies. Bring the whole lot to the simmer and cook for 15 minutes.

Stir well then ladle into the warm sterilised jars. Seal and label when the jars have cooled. Keep for 4–6 weeks before eating. Stored in a cool place, away from direct sunlight, these pickles will keep for up to a year (if you don't eat them first!).

STORING YOUR VEG

Blanching (or scalding) vegetables before freezing them halts the enzyme actions, which ensures that flavour, colour and texture don't deteriorate while they're stored in the freezer. It is easy to do and I tend to do a batch, so that I can get a good number of veggies blanched in a short time using the same pan of water. All vegetables are suitable for blanching. If freezer space is limited I tend to limit my store to those crops that are either expensive or hard to come by during the winter months.

YOU WILL NEED
your largest saucepan
blanching basket or colander
slotted spoon
clean, dry tea towel
tray
freezer-proof bags or boxes

My peas and beans have not been sprayed or over-handled, so I find they don't need a wash. Shell broad beans and garden peas but French beans and mangetout peas can blanched whole. Empty pods can then either be added to the compost area or set aside (they can be added to the blanching water after the session along with an onion and any other vegetable trimmings to make a veggie stock – see page 170). Anyway, back to the blanching. Fill your largest saucepan with water to within about 5cm (2 inches) of the top of the pan and bring it to a fast boil. While it's coming to the boil, fill a clean sink with cold water and throw in a few ice cubes if you have them: the colder the better.

Once the water is boiling, drop in a number of beans. I find a half-filled colander or blanching basket is just about right. If you blanch too many beans in one go, they cool the water down too quickly and don't get the swift scald required to blanch them effectively. Blanch for just 1 minute, then take the pan to the sink and use a slotted spoon to lift them from the boiling water, drain to remove as much excess water as possible then drop the peas or beans into the sink of icy water. If you used a blanching basket or colander this is much easier – just plunge the basket or colander into the cold water.

Replace the pan on the hob, and quickly return it to the boil ready for the next batch, rather like a production line!

Swirl the beans around in the icy-cold water then, once cold, remove using the slotted spoon and lay on a clean, dry tea towel. Once dried lay them on a tray and open-freeze for 1 hour until firmed up. Transfer to freezer-proof bags or boxes and you have perfect home-grown frozen veggies to enjoy when the season is long finished.

I don't refresh the boiling blanching water. In fact, after a long blanching session the water may be a gorgeous colour and I use it as a base for a veggie stock (see page 170) – as mentioned above, use the discarded pods too.

The cold water may need more ice cubes or a cold-water top-up between batches, as it will warm up after the addition of scalded beans.

Frozen vegetables will keep up to a year in the freezer.

COOKING YOUR FROZEN VEG

Most people, whether they grow their own veggies or not, have frozen vegetables of some kind in the freezer. I have written in some detail about blanching veggies to make them suitable for freezing on pages 151–2 and here is a little note about how I go on to cook them, which has them tasting as though they have just been picked fresh from the garden (with no hint of mushiness or 'freezer' odour).

Frozen peas are a great go-to frozen veg: I throw a frozen handful into casseroles and stews at the end of cooking to add some colour and zing. They thaw easily, need little or no cooking, and add extra veggies and flavour, as well as a colourful garnish if you don't have fresh parsley available.

Cook peas, broad beans, French beans very briefly in order to retain their texture and flavour. Pop them straight from the freezer into a large saucepan that will offer your veggies room to move around then fill the pan with cold water. The water helps to thaw the veggies and melt off any ice clusters that may have formed around them. Pour the whole lot through a colander so that only the drained veggies remain and there are no icy clusters or freezer odour. Add a knob of butter to the pan and no more than 2 tablespoons of cold water, place over a medium heat and – when the butter melts – add the drained veggies. Cover and cook for 2–3 minutes, then strain off the scant amount of liquid, add a little seasoning and serve. The veggies have a glossy finish with excellent flavour and colour, are not mushy or overcooked and taste absolutely delicious.

POWDERY MILDEW AND FUNGUS FIX

When growing courgettes – and I strongly recommend that you do – it is important to keep them well watered, with good air circulation. Strong, healthy, well-watered plants will often resist the fungus, but when the weather is damp and humid you may notice a white/grey powdery coating on the leaves of your courgettes.

Powdery mildew is easy to detect. It looks as though the leaves have been sprayed pale grey. It is a fungus that thrives in damp conditions and is destructive too: left untreated, it will cause leaves to shrivel and die. The leaves become distorted and if the fungus is allowed to spread then it can affect the flowers and fruits. Powdery mildew also adores the leaves of roses, cucumbers, apples, blackcurrants, marrows, peas and sweet peas, though courgettes in my experience seem to be the most affected.

I have found this quick and easy-to-make spray to be effective at treating and controlling powdery mildew on roses, cucumbers and courgettes and it halted an attack of black spot on my roses. As I understand it, the bicarb solution creates an alkaline environment on the leaf which makes it difficult for the powdery mildew and black spot fungus to survive and thrive.

The quantities below make enough to treat 3–4 large courgette plants. It is a fairly gentle spray, and not one that will hurt insects (especially if sprayed in the evening when they are asleep), I repeat the spray once a week until I see that new leaves that appear are free of any sign of the fungus.

YOU WILL NEED

1 tsp bicarbonate of soda

500ml (17fl oz) bottle with spray attachment

350ml water (100ml/3½fl oz warm and 250ml/8fl oz cold)

3 drops eco-friendly washing-up liquid

Measure the bicarbonate of soda straight into a spray bottle then add about 100ml (3½fl oz) warm water. Shake the bottle to help mix the ingredients, then add the washing-up liquid and the rest of the water. Shake and it is ready for use. Strong, healthy, well-watered plants will often resist the fungus but at first signs of an attack spray well in the evening when the weather is still. Repeat weekly if necessary.

HARVESTING AND FREEZING SOFT FRUITS AND BERRIES

There is so much produce at this time of year and nothing equals the taste of home-grown organic veggies. If you grow your own soft fruits such as blackcurrants, strawberries, redcurrants, white currants and gooseberries, they will often be ready at the same time. Fortunately, nowadays they can be easily frozen. Before freezers, fruits were dried, bottled and made into jams yet now, as well as preserving them in these traditional ways, we can easily freeze them. See table on page 304 and tip on page 61 for how to keep your berries fresh for at least two weeks without freezing.

When harvesting soft fruits for freezing, I try to handle them only the once. Ripe soft berries can easily burst, bruise or damage, so when I'm picking them I take with me not a bowl or basket but a tray that will then slot straight into the freezer. I try to harvest in the morning when the weather and the berries are dry, before the sun heats up them up and makes them even softer, then carefully pop each one onto the tray. Once the tray has a single layer I take it straight to the freezer. After an hour the berries are firm and can be packed into bags or boxes, resulting in them being undamaged and therefore free flowing and easy to use from frozen.

Small jewel-like berries such as blackcurrants, white currants and redcurrants grow in hanging clusters of as many as 15 berries resembling a mass of brightly coloured dangly earrings. After pulling down on a cluster to release it from the main branch, I take a table fork and with the cluster of berries in one hand and the fork in the other, I insert the prongs of the fork through the mass of little stalks and simply pull down, releasing the berries from the stalks and straight onto the tray. There is minimum berry damage, and it is quicker than trying to pick each berry by hand. Again, once there is a single layer of berries on the tray, they go straight into the freezer.

BREAKFAST BERRY JAM

Strawberries do not freeze well on their own – they go very mushy – but they can be enjoyed during the winter months, tasting fresh and zingy by preserving them in this delicious Breakfast Berry Jam. I use any mix of soft fruits for this – sometimes strawberries on their own, sometimes a combination of whatever is available to make up the weight.

I'm trying not to show off here but in my drive towards self-sufficiency and seasonality, I resist buying fresh soft fruits and berries during the winter months. Apart from the expense, there is the packaging and the added environmental pressure of food miles. Out-of-season imported berries may travel by air to the UK in refrigerated containers from as far away as Peru in order to satisfy our desire, rather than need, to have fresh fruits with our yoghurt, cereal or muesli at breakfast. Wherever you live in this world, imported produce is never going to taste as fresh and delicious as those grown closer to home. In order to make foods fit to travel I am sure too that they will have had to be sprayed and treated with all manner of substances in order to keep them fresh and looking perfect.

This refined-sugar-free Breakfast Berry Jam, stored in the freezer, keeps me going all winter and right until the next year's harvest. I make about three jars at a time, and when I run out, I turn to my stocks of frozen berries to make another batch.

I urge you to make this – I would never be without it now – and if you are wanting to do your bit for our planet but don't grow fruit at home, why not buy gluts of in-season fresh berries to make this, rather than buying the imported fresh alternatives. It is safe, by the way, to thaw and then refreeze the berries, because they will have been cooked.

Makes 3 x 1 lb jars

YOU WILL NEED

lemon zester

large bowl

potato masher

large saucepan

wooden spoon

jam funnel (or jug), if needed

3 or 4 clean 450g (1 lb) glass jars which will be suitable for
freezing as long as the jam is given sufficient space to
expand, or use plastic freezer-proof containers

500g (1lb 2oz) seasonal berries – a mix of strawberries,
raspberries, redcurrants, blackcurrants, blueberries,
blackberries and small gooseberries (or use frozen mixed
berries)

finely grated zest and juice of 1 orange or 1 lemon

50g (1¾oz) honey

2 tsp vanilla extract

1–2 tsp ground cinnamon

Place the washed fruits, lemon or orange zest and juice into
a large bowl and use a potato masher to break everything down
so that the juices run but the fruit still has large lumps. If
using frozen fruits, see instructions below.

Remove half of the fresh berry pulp and add it to a large
saucepan then add the honey. Bring to a fast boil and cook
for 3 minutes, stirring from time to time with a wooden spoon
to prevent the mixture sticking to the bottom of the pan.
Transfer the thickened, hot bubbling fruits to the bowl with
the other half of the pulp. Stir well and add the vanilla and

cinnamon, then transfer to clean jars or freezer-proof containers, using a funnel if necessary. Seal and label.

If freezing in glass jars, don't fill them right to the top but  leave about 2cm (¾ inch) headroom so that there is space for the jam to expand as it freezes (then the glass won't crack). Pop into the freezer.

Thaw in the fridge for 12 hours or so before using. Once thawed, it will keep for 7–10 days in the fridge.

If using frozen berries, place them all in a saucepan and leave to thaw at room temperature. Once thawed it will not be necessary to mash them because the fruits will be soft anyway and will have produced juices, so simply add the honey, lemon/orange zest and juice then bring the whole lot to a fast boil for 3 minutes, stirring from time to time. Take off the heat, stir through the vanilla and cinnamon then allow to cool before transferring to the glass jars or plastic containers.

LATE SUMMER

L ate summer is the time when many veggies and fruits come into their own as they mature and ripen. The gardens, shops, markets and supermarkets will have an abundance of in-season fruits and veggies and even the non-gardener may want to take the opportunity to buy these at a good price and store them ready to be enjoyed during the lean months.

Sow Cabbages

Between now and early autumn is the time to sow spring cabbages – these are really fantastic because they will be ready to harvest in early spring the next year when there is very little else to harvest and fresh veggies are expensive in the shops. Unlike sowing in spring, summer sown crops are very swift. Seeds planted outside one day, watered in well because the soil will be dry, not needing any shelter or protection from the elements, will be showing their first pairs of leaves in little more than a week. These seedlings, once they then go on to produce their first adult leaves can be grown on to about six inches in height and then given their final growing spot where they will bravely stand up to the winter weather.

Sweetcorn

As sweetcorn plants grow tall (1.8–2.5 metres/6–8 feet), they will reveal pointed clusters of tassels at the very tops which over the next few weeks will open out and be covered in fine pollen. Lower down the plant will be beautifully fine pale-green silks growing on the stems at the places where the cobs of corn are beginning to develop. The tassels at the very top pollinate the silks below and, once this happens, the silks will turn from pale green to pale yellow, then die off and will turn brown to indicate that the corn kernels inside the cobs are ready to harvest, next season.

I began growing sweetcorn several years ago and every year they fascinate me. I love them and always include them in my planting plans. The majestic tall plants resemble no other vegetable in my garden. I have never had to pollinate sweetcorn myself (I didn't even realise it was a thing until I read advice online about removing tassels and hand pollinating the silks below); I find that at the slightest breath of wind, the pollen-loaded tassels sway gently, giving off a puff of powder pollen which then scatters from plant to plant, pollinating the corn kernels below.

Reduce the Rasps!

The summer fruiting canes will be finished and the Autumn Bliss varieties will take over, bearing often much bigger berries which will take you right up to early winter. I have even harvested a number of (admittedly fairly feeble) berries on Christmas Eve. The summer fruiting varieties can be tidied up at this stage. You will need a good pair of secateurs to remove the tatty-looking canes that had provided the berries. Cut them right at the base, undo any ties on wires and remove the whole lot.

By doing this, the fresh, green, tall, new growth which has been pushing upwards will be given lots more space and light to continue building up strength ready to provide next year's fruits. Once the old has been removed, in with the new! Allow the four strongest new canes to remain and cut down any more than that at ground level. Secure these remaining four with ties onto the existing wires to stabilise them and protect them from autumn and winter winds and weather. Any very tall canes – I have had some much taller than me – I leave for now then cut down to about 1.5 metres (5 foot) in height once the leaves have fallen off in the autumn.

Leeks

What were spindly specimens will now be standing tall and resplendent and I may harvest the odd one or two but as there is so much else to harvest I prefer to leave these beauties as they are. They will withstand everything that autumn and winter throws at them and any that I have left will always be there as a fresh veg supply.

Parsnips

This season's crop should be looking gorgeous, with huge bushy green leaves, and by the end of the month you may want to try one or two, but I tend to leave them in the ground for early winter use.

If you have grown some of the previous season's parsnips for seed as mentioned earlier (see page 47), the seed heads will now be formed. The very tall parsnip plant (1.8–2.5 metres /6–8 feet tall) will have developed upside-down umbrella-type flowers which then give way to tiny green seeds, then turning a caramel colour. At this point (during late summer/early autumn) the dried flower heads can be harvested.

Carefully remove the seed head with scissors then stand the seed head upside down in a large paper bag or pot and leave in a warm dry place – the shed is perfect. As they dry, the seeds then drop off into the bag or pot and can then be stored over winter in labelled paper bags or envelopes. There you are – free seeds! More than you can ever use. The original plants can then be uplifted, cut into 15–23cm (6–9 inch) lengths and composted. Don't be limited to parsnips – when you see seed heads appear around the garden and want to increase your stocks of veggie, plant or flowers – give it a go!

Trim Mint and Chives

Any of your herb plants that are looking leggy or brown will benefit from a late summer haircut. Rather than deplete the whole plant I tend to give a half cut, leaving a few straggly leaves for harvesting now and then. New growth will appear in a few days and, once this is showing and is large enough to harvest, I will cut the other half.

The Luffa Gourd Challenge

The plant continues to grow upwards and onwards – many clusters of male flowers and yes still no females until one evening I see one! Hurrah – are things looking up? The next day I see more female flowers – maybe six or eight in total and each one with the beginnings of tiny luffa formations too – each about 5cm (2 inches) long. Could we be in business?

Without going into a panic, I did some reading and research online and discovered that the female flowers need to be hand pollinated. Some growers use paint brushes, dabbing first the male flower then transferring the pollen over to the female. Never having done this before and not really thinking this was necessary because with doors and windows open in my greenhouse there were many flying insects around. Without a handy paintbrush I simply removed a male flower with scissors and dabbled it around two of the female flowers.

I left alone the other female flowers that were present as a kind of experiment. I decided to leave the pollination of the rest of them to the insects in order to ascertain whether my intervention was at all necessary.

A week later – my two hand pollinated luffas were storming ahead, doubled in size whereas the ones I had left to nature had withered and dropped off from the plant as before.

I had just two babies – now to do my best for them. Astonishingly in just over two weeks my two fruits had grown to 36cm (14 inches) in length and 7.5–10cm (3 to 4 inches) at their widest point and looked like two enormous cucumbers yet with a dull and paler skin. These fruits were heavy too and when I walked into the greenhouse one morning to see them both fallen to the floor – yet thankfully still attached to the plant – I realised I needed to offer a helping hand. I popped each heavy fruit into a netting bag and hung the bag from a hook above my head attached to the greenhouse wooden roof. The bags now took the weight of the fruits rather than the plant.

Compost Conscious

While enjoying the fruits of our labours we will also be deciding what to maybe do differently next year. Maybe the peas didn't do so well so I make a note (in the diary! See page 20) and think about a change in variety or change of position next year. Remember also, as crops finish, that you will have a bountiful supply of 'wet' compost material. There will be weeds too and extra grass clippings. Be mindful of the salad sandwich (see page 32) and refrain from piling too many wet ingredients into the compost without also adding some layers of dry – even a sheet of cardboard or paper will do.

Equally, the weather may be dry, so watering the compost bin when adding more layers is a good idea at this time of the year to keep it going if it is dry and, if you have a compost thermometer, stick it into the pile for a fun reading. It should be working hard.

Check In On Your Pots

Even crops grown in pots will probably provide more than you can manage in one go at this time of year. Tomatoes, cucumbers and courgettes, once they get going, never seem to stop – in fact most veggies will be doing so well just now that the first thoughts are to give away your surplus. However, there are freezer-friendly ideas and preserving recipes for just about any fruit and veg, and if you want to continue to enjoy your fresh produce for weeks rather than days, visit the table on page 303 and enjoy your fresh home-grown veg for longer than just a week or so.

Even though a pot or container of salad leaves, radish or spring onions may have been used up, there is still time to sow another batch and – unlike sowing back in spring – these seedlings will appear in a matter of days. If you have the space, sowing every three weeks even in seed trays will ensure summer-long crops.

Pot-grown peppers and chillies again will be developing fruit: though still green in colour the fruit will be large and looking luscious and will begin to lighten in colour as the season changes. Following the pale lilac flowers will emerge the deep purple, shiny aubergine. What may appear nothing larger than a golf ball will in a matter of days be the size of a small pear and hey-ho – soon it will be ready to harvest.

Split your Bumper Supply of Spring Flowering Bulbs

Earlier on in the book (page 92) I mention removing tubs and pots of spring flowering bulbs to an 'out of the way' place to finish drying out. I still give them a drink of water from time to time during periods of dry weather, but by now the tops are completely dried and may have even blown away and disappeared. The pots can be top-dressed with a little more fresh compost or leaf mould or the bulbs can be taken from the pots. If you have the time, the inclination and interest, and like the thought of more free bulbs, splitting the bulbs is a great pastime. Actually, all spring flowering bulbs enjoy being split every three years or so. It improves their performance and flowering.

I like to do this on a warm sunny afternoon.

Dig down into your pot with your hands and begin to reveal your bulbs. The first thing you will notice is that there are lots more than you originally planted. The bulbs, whether they are daffodils or tulips, will have doubled and many will come out of the compost in little pairs, joined at the hip. After rubbing them clean of any residual soil or compost with gloved hands, set them out on a tray to dry off. Those bulbs that are doubled-up can easily be separated by simply breaking them in two. Just like onions, the bulbs will need to dry out. Once dry to the touch, they can be stored in boxes, paper bags or netting sacks and kept in a dry shed or garage ready to be planted in mid to late autumn into new pots, tubs or into the ground (see page 219).

One year, I split a container which had flowered a mass of 'tete-a-tete' mini daffodils the previous spring. I had what seemed like hundreds of little bulbs which I then planted into small pots to be given as Christmas gifts to family and friends. I bought pretty planters to pop the pots into and they all loved them. This is a great free gift of nature.

FOR THE LOVE OF STRAWBERRIES

My lovely strawberries having flowered well earlier, begin to fruit from early summer and when, following a number of weeks, I harvest the last of the berries it is time to give the plants a make-over, along with some care and attention.

I begin by removing my netted frame that had been used to keep the birds off my precious fruits – that will not be needed again until next spring. The first thing I notice is that the whole bed, plants and all, looks weary and unruly. The plants have a number of yellowed leaves and also, because they have been covered over for some time, large weeds have taken hold between the plants. The first job is a thorough weeding of the bed.

Next, I take a look at what is going on. When fruiting stops, the plants begin to throw out runners. These look like green stalks emerging from the centre of the plant and they grow very quickly, easily reaching 30–36cm (12–14 inches) in length in no time. At the end of this runner a tiny cluster of leaves will then emerge. It is now decision time – do I need more strawberry plants? If I am in need of more plants, I will allow the runners to continue to grow, and if I am happy with the stocks I have then it's haircut time.

When my plants are young (less than three years old), I take my scissors and cut the whole plant down to a stubble about 2.5cm (1 inch) high. By cutting the strawberry right back and effectively giving it a prune, I am preventing it using energy to create runners and new plants. Over the next few weeks, as the weather is still warm, the plant will soon develop lush new green leaves. The plants will look tidy and compact, ready for autumn and a dormant winter, and will be healthy and ready to fruit again next year.

With older strawberry plants it is better to have new stocks ready to replace them. This is really easy to do – in fact they do it themselves. After fruiting, rather than giving the plants a haircut as mentioned above, instead allow them to grow their long runners. These long stalks will develop a cluster of new leaves at the end which if left unchecked will grow – this is a new baby plant. If you are wanting to replenish or increase your stock of strawberries, then allow your plants to grow these runners. The little end clusters of leaves will then start to grow roots and at this stage the runners will find a place to root themselves (but not necessarily where you want them). Keep a close eye on the runners and get ahead by filling as many 7.5cm (3 inch) pots as you have runners with compost in advance. When the airborne runners begin to grow little roots, dig a little hole in the ground and place the compost-filled pot in the hole to prevent the wind from blowing it over. It's important to keep watch and catch the plant before it has taken root itself next to its mum. Place the rooting runner into the pot and secure it with a piece of 'u'-shaped wire to keep it firmly in place until the roots take hold. The small plant is still attached to the mother and needs time to establish itself and grow further roots.

After a few weeks, if you lift the pot from the ground, you will see that the runner is well rooted and at this stage the new strawberry plant can be safely detached from its mother. Use scissors to cut the umbilical cord close to the main plant and again close to the baby plant. These new baby strawberry plants will stay in their pots outside from now, through the autumn and winter, ready to take up residence in a permanent bed in early spring (see page 50).

'WASTE NOTHING' STOCK

Whether growing in containers, an allotment or a designated garden veggie patch, after all the hard work planning, caring and watering we can use far more than just the finished delicious veggies. Having used no harmful pesticides or insecticides, chemical fertilisers or any nasties whatsoever, every morsel can be enjoyed.

Washed potato, turnip and beetroot peelings, carrot tops, tomato stalks, parsley stalks, onion skins – in fact anything other than rhubarb leaves or green potatoes as these are poisonous – can be popped into a bag and then into the freezer to be used to make a wholesome veggie stock when the bag is full enough.

YOU WILL NEED
freezer-proof reusable plastic box
large casserole dish or stock pan
sieve

variety of frozen vegetable trimmings
a few black peppercorns (optional)
1 or 2 bay leaves (optional)

Put your full bag of trimmings in a large casserole dish or stock pan and fill about three-quarters full of cold water – or if you have been blanching veg for the freezer (see page 151), use the pan of pale green liquid rather than pour it down the drain. Add black peppercorns and bay leaves, if you like. Bring to the boil, cover and simmer for 20–30 minutes.

Leave to cool in the pan before straining and adding the trimmings to the compost.

Use the dark golden, flavoursome liquid in soups, stews and casseroles. It will keep for up to 5 days in the fridge, or can be frozen for up to 6 months.

TIP: Alter If you are struggling for freezer space, veggie trimmings can be dried in a dehydrator or a low oven (as low as your oven will go, mine is about 80-100°C/Gas Mark ¼/200°F), blitzed to a powder, then stored to be used as a homemade veggie stock, rehydrated with boiling water. 1 tablespoon of powder to 300ml (10fl oz) boiling water will give the perfect stock base to your stews, casseroles, pasta dishes, soups, etc. without the excess salt, preservatives or colourings often contained in stock cubes or shop bought bouillon.

TOMATO PASSATA

We have tomatoes! Every day there are more! We eat many of my tomatoes fresh – I love them – and turn the misshapen or split fruits into this yummy passata (a thick tomato sauce) which I use through the winter in casseroles, soups, pasta sauce, pizza, moussaka (or in any recipe that calls for a tin of tomatoes). Even if you don't grow your own tomatoes, they are in season now and such good value in the shops it is worth buying them just to make this!

Tomatoes don't freeze well as they are – the skins split and the insides turn mushy – but sometimes if I don't have the time to use them straight away I may pop a bagful into the freezer to use for frying or make this passata later.

Makes 1.5kg (3lb 5oz)

YOU WILL NEED
sharp knife
very large saucepan or casserole dish
6 x 450g (1lb) glass jars with screw-top lids or some clean
    plastic tubs
stick blender (optional)
tea towel or cloth

2kg (4lb 8oz) ripe tomatoes (including any split, misshapen
    or wonky ones)
3 tbsp olive oil or rapeseed oil
2 onions, chopped
1½ tbsp dried mixed herbs
1 tsp sugar
4 garlic cloves, chopped
salt and pepper

Start by skinning the larger tomatoes. It's not essential on the smaller ones. This might seem a bit tedious, but it is worth it:

tomato skin doesn't break down during cooking and those on very large or split tomatoes are particularly tough. Use a sharp knife to cut a cross in the bottom of each tomato at its base. Place the tomatoes in a large heatproof bowl then pour over boiling water, enough to just cover. Leave for about 5 minutes, then pour off the water. When the tomatoes are cool enough to handle, carefully peel off the skins, starting at the base of the tomato where you have made the cross. They should come off easily, especially if the tomatoes are really ripe.

TIP: I used to pop tomato skins into the compost bin, but not anymore! I dry them on kitchen paper, lay them on a cooling rack and simply leave them on a sunny windowsill until dry and crisp. Blitzed to a powder in a food processor, then stored in a reused spice jar, I have another layer of flavour to add to soups, stews, casseroles and pasta. Use 1 teaspoon in place of 1 tablespoon of tomato paste to thicken and add flavour to your recipes. Try this with pepper skins too.

Heat the oil in a very large saucepan or casserole dish over a medium heat, then add the chopped onions and fry gently for about 10 minutes until they have softened. Add the dried herbs, sugar and garlic and stir well before adding the tomatoes. I tend to cut the tomatoes in half as I add them to the pan, so the juices can quickly be released into the sauce. Turn up the heat, stir well and bring everything to a bubble, then turn the heat down to a gentle simmer and cook, uncovered, for 2 hours, stirring occasionally.

After 2 hours, your tomatoes will have reduced down and thickened. You can store the sauce as it is though I prefer a really smooth tomato sauce and give it a quick blitz with a stick blender. Season to taste and leave to cool in the pan then freeze in re-usable plastic tubs or reuse cream or yoghurt pots that have a lid. The passata will freeze for up to 1 year. When ready to use, thaw in the fridge overnight or at room temperature for 2–3 hours.

If you're short on freezer space, you can bottle the sauce in sterilised jars (see page 150 for sterilising method). Once the sauce is bottled and you've screwed on the lids, lay a small tea towel or cloth in the base of your largest casserole dish or stock pan then set the sealed jars onto the cloth, tucking the cloth between each glass jar so that they don't touch each other and bang together. Cover the whole lot in cold water and make sure the water covers the jars. Bring to the boil and simmer for just 10 minutes then turn off the heat, put a lid on the pan and leave the jars in the hot water for 40 minutes. This final process forms a seal inside the jar which will ensure the sauce stays fresh. Dry the jars and store in a cool place for up to a year. Once opened, if a whole jar is not used – the remainder will keep in the fridge for a week or so.

BEETROOT

When beetroot looks no larger than a tidy row of dark purple tennis balls, it's harvest time. If the ground is moist the roots will lift easily, but often in late summer the conditions are hard and dry. If this is the case, I take a hand fork or trowel in one hand to gently ease the beetroot while pulling on the bunch of leaves above using the other hand. Don't be tempted to cut the leaves from the beets: a simple twist and they will come away all together leaving a short stalk stubble, the roots won't be split or damaged and the dark red dye won't leak.

There is a mass of foliage with beetroot. I compost some of it, and use the very best leaves – those not too big but not too small – as I would spinach. They're delicious.

To keep my gorgeous beetroot in good condition so that my kitchen is well stocked during the winter months, I store them in a box of sand. The sand keeps the beetroot cool, damp and fresh – it's the same principle as the damp cloths in the salad compartment of the fridge (see page 60) – though if I stored my beetroot this way there wouldn't be space for anything else.

I fill a deep wooden box with a 5cm (2 inch) layer of sand in the base. The roots and leaf stubble of the beetroots are still intact, any soil has been rubbed off, then I place them neatly, not touching each other, in a single layer in the box, on their sides. I add a further layer of sand to cover, repeat with a second layer of beetroot and sand, and then a third. After a final covering of sand, I label the box and leave it in the garage. This method can also be used for carrots.

Fill your box with beets and sand when you're actually in the place that they are going to be stored – a garage or shed. The first time I did this, by the time I had filled my box with around 40 beetroot and the added sand – I couldn't lift it!

Grandma's Beetroot Pickle

For those growing beetroot for pickling, this recipe is my grandma's and it's my go-to pickle every year. The only change

I have made over the years has been to toast the pickling spices to bring out their full flavour.

Makes 5–6 x 450g (1lb) jars

YOU WILL NEED
large saucepan with a lid
6 x 450g (1lb) glass jars with screw-top lids
rubber gloves (optional)
small frying pan
medium saucepan
sieve

2kg (4lb 8oz) beetroot, washed
5 tbsp pickling spice
1.4 litres (2½ pints) malt vinegar
200g (7oz) light brown sugar
salt

Place the washed beetroots in an even layer in a large saucepan then add sufficient water to barely cover. Bring to the boil, cover and simmer for 30–40 minutes until tender or – to save time and energy – cook for just 10 minutes on high pressure in a pressure cooker. The benefits of pressure cooking is that the water in the vessel need only be a couple of centimeters (an inch) deep in the bottom of the pan. You will know when your beetroots are cooked and tender because the point of a vegetable knife will slide through easily.

Sterilise your jars according to the method on page 150.

Drain the cooked beetroot and leave to cool, then cut off the top stubble and the root and rub off the skins. Note that the beetroot will stain your hands – I wear rubber gloves to do this job.

Place the pickling spice in a dry frying pan and toast gently over a low heat. You will know when the spices are roasting as you will smell the wonderful perfume and aroma being released from the seeds. My shop-bought pickling spice also contains bay leaf pieces and small whole chillies. Remove these from the mix before toasting as they will quickly burn. Pop the bay and chilli into a medium saucepan.

Once toasted, transfer the spices immediately from the hot pan to the medium saucepan so that they don't burn in the residual heat of the frying pan. Add the vinegar and sugar and place over a gentle heat until the sugar has dissolved, then turn the heat and boil for 5 minutes.

Slice the beetroot about 0.5cm (¼ inch) thick into the clean sterilised jars, then add a pinch of the salt. Strain the hot vinegar to remove the spices and pour it over the beetroot in the jars. Spoon back in some of the spices (or leave them out, if you prefer). Seal and wait a month for the flavours to mature before eating. This is a great edible gift for Christmas! Pickled beetroot can be stored in a cool dark place (pantry or cupboard) for a year and once opened I keep the jar in the fridge for up to six weeks.

CUCUMBERS

If you are growing cucumbers, they will be coming thick and fast, very much like courgettes. They need lots of water and I give them a weekly feed, just like tomatoes, and – when the weather is very hot – a fine water spray is much welcomed.

Harvest them regularly – I keep family and friends well supplied at this time of the year. Wrap them in damp towels in the fridge in order to extend their shelf life (see page 59).

Cucumber Pickle

I make a cucumber pickle every year. It always goes down well at Christmas and is a firm favourite with the whole family and, I may add, is a great edible gift idea for friends. It's easy to make too, and preserves your perfect organically grown veggies. It keeps for a year and works brilliantly with cold meats, sausages and cheese. For extra flavour, try adding a large spoonful to your favourite casserole or savoury pie filling.

Preparation needs to start the day before, to allow the excess moisture to release from the cucumber slices.

Makes 5 x 450g (1lb) jars

YOU WILL NEED
food processor, mandoline or sharp vegetable knife
large colander
lipped tray or dish (to catch juices)
plate and weights
5 x 450g (1lb) glass jars
large casserole dish or preserving pan
slotted spoon

3 large cucumbers, thinly sliced (skin on, washed)
3 large onions (try 2 white and 1 red), peeled and thinly
  sliced

50g (1¾oz) salt
570ml (19fl oz) white distilled vinegar
450g (1lb) soft light brown sugar
1 tsp ground turmeric
1 tbsp mustard seeds

Use a mandoline or food processor with a slicer attachment for the cucumber and onions if you have one, for super-speedy slicing. Alternatively, use a steady hand and a sharp vegetable knife to cut them both into thin slices.

Layer the sliced cucumbers and onions in a large colander, sprinkling the salt across the layers as you go. Place the colander on a large lipped tray or dish and lay a plate over the top covered with a weight (a tin of beans works well). Leave overnight in a cool place – the salt will draw the juices from the cucumbers and onions and you will see the pool on the tray the next morning.

When ready to make the pickle, sterilise your jars (see page 150).

Pour away the liquid on the tray from the cucumbers and onions – there's no need to rinse the veggies.

Pour the vinegar into a large casserole dish or preserving pan. Add the sugar and spices and stir over a medium heat until the sugar dissolves. Bring the whole lot to the boil then drop in the drained cucumber and onion and boil for just 1 minute. Use a slotted spoon to remove the cucumber and onion from the vinegar (or pour through a colander and catch the vinegar in a second saucepan) and place into the hot sterilised jars. Pack the onions and cucumbers in quite tightly, leaving only a small space of about 1cm (½ inch) at the top of the jar.

Bring the vinegar back to the boil and let it bubble for 15 minutes to reduce down, then pour into the cucumber- and onion-filled jars. Fill them right to the top to cover the contents in the pickling liquid. Seal the jars with the lids while hot and label when cold. Keep for 1 month before serving (if you can wait, that is – I have eaten them earlier and they are yummy, but by waiting the pickle has time to mellow and develop). This pickle keeps for a year in a cool pantry and once opened I keep it in the fridge for 4-6 weeks.

Transfer any leftover pickling vinegar to a vinegar bottle and keep it handy in the cupboard – it is delicious on chips!

PLANT FEED WITH ADDED BENEFIT

Late summer tends to be party time for caterpillars so, if you have sprout plants and cabbages, now is the time to keep an eye out. Little round clusters of pale cream eggs often about the size of a drawing pin can be spotted on the underside of large leaves. These can easily be rubbed off without the need for harmful sprays. As I mention on page 54, I prefer to net off sprouts, cabbages and kale and choose to grow early summer varieties of cauliflower that are harvested before the cabbage whites arrive.

Plants love this liquid feed even though it smells awful to us. When I decided to add a little clove-bud oil I thought it smelled even worse! Plants are able to absorb essential elements through their leaves (foliage). After reading that plants love a nettle feed, and that clove bud oil is an insect deterrent, I made this mix because I wanted to give my veggies an organic feed while at the same time trying to keep butterflies off my cabbages (it not only repels butterflies and other flying insects, it also controls aphids). This recipe isn't new – I included it in my book *Clean & Green*. I wanted to repeat it however because I saw for myself the effect it had on the wellbeing and health of my cabbages, how it was a natural deterrent to the butter-flies and the calming and satisfying effect it had on me!

I sat one sunny afternoon watching the outcome of a simple experiment: I had two rows of savoy cabbages, resplendent with their huge hearts and dark green frilly frocks. The rows of perfect veggies seemed too good to eat but I removed the netting covers and harvested one anyway and then noticed a number of cabbage white butterflies came zooming into my line of sight from nowhere! I decided to spray and feed just half the row, leaving the other half untouched. I then sat there to simply watch what happened. You can probably guess the outcome – the sprayed cabbages were rejected! If you have every watched butterflies, they seem to bob around in circles, obviously checking out, sniffing and assessing the best egg-laying place – it is really quite calming. These butterflies – about four in all – were dancing and swaying in the sunshine but once within a few inches of the stinky spray were upwards and onwards. Here was the proof I needed that clove-bud oil was indeed an insect deterrent. Even though they circled them more than once, they didn't set foot on my cabbages – instead they began to concentrate on the unsprayed ones. I shooed them away and was in there with the spray bottle and it was back on with my nets.

Makes about 500ml (17fl oz) spray

YOU WILL NEED
rubber gloves
scissors
60g (2¼oz) nettles (leaves and stalks)
clean, old plastic tub or similar with a lid
600ml (20fl oz) cold water (rainwater is ideal)
old fine tea strainer
1-litre (34fl oz) bottle with spray attachment
1–2 drops eco-friendly washing-up liquid
6 drops clove-bud oil

Wearing gloves, harvest the nettles with scissors. Select the young leaves because they contain more nitrogen that is quickly broken down in water. The leaves need to be 5–7cm (2–3 inches) long. Pop them into a plastic tub that has a lid. I buy my bicarbonate of soda in 5kg (11lb) tubs and this container, complete with handle and lid, is perfect. Pour over the cold water (or rainwater), stir and push the nettles into the water using a gloved hand. Pop the lid on and leave outside and forget about it for at least a week (2 weeks is even better), stirring maybe once or twice during that time. I left one lot for over a month because I forgot about it.

When ready to use (and I suggest you do this outside), take off the lid, give it a stir and the smell will send you reeling – it really is awful, but plants love it! Strain off the leaves, using simply the lid as an aid, then strain again using an old fine tea strainer (the nettles will be a welcome addition to the compost heap). Fill the spray bottle with the foul-smelling liquid, then add the eco-friendly washing-up liquid and clove-bud oil. Give it a good shake then spray away! I tend to make a mix and use it though I have also kept it in the shed for several weeks and used the rest. At the end of the season I pour any remaining onto the compost and clean out the bottles ready for use next year.

I avoid using this spray on my vegetables just before I want to eat them, though the spray will readily wash off so it's not a big deal if you do.

LONG LIVE LAVENDER

Another natural pest deterrent – and a plant that we all know and love for its fragrant and edible flowers which can be dried and popped into little bags – is lavender. Many gardens have a lavender bush that may once have been perfectly shaped, lush and bushy and bearing the pale lilac perfumed flowers on long stalks.

It may have then been left unattended, probably because it is one of those plants that you think just keeps going. Eventually, however, lavender starts to look unruly and woody, producing fewer flowers, and many gardeners may think it has had its day. I have a whole row of miniature lavender bushes which edge a pathway and for a number of years they were neat and compact, bearing gorgeous flowers. For the first few years I pruned them every summer, soon after the flowers had faded, and the next year they grew nicely. After a number of years, when the plants became woody and leggy, with some having retained their shape while others looked rather bare, I thought maybe it was time to dig them out and start again, as some gardening books suggested a lavender plant only lives about five years so. Instead, I replaced my stock with cuttings. When I saw how much young lavender plants were to buy – and I needed many of them – the sensible thing to do was to take cuttings from the stock I had. This is very easy to do and it works for all sorts of woody-stalked plants like rosemary, lilac and sage. Cut a length of about 15cm (6 inches), remove the leaves from the bottom half of the stalk, dip them in hormone rooting powder and pop three stems each into a 7.5cm (3 inch) pot of compost.

In fact, when I looked closely at the ground surrounding the plants, I could see that some lavender seed had already 'self-set' and I had a number of free little plants already growing, though not exactly where I wanted them to be. Some had even managed to take root at the edge of the lawn and between cracks in the path. I wanted to nurture these little heroes and just needed to carefully lift and transfer them to pots and – once they had grown in stature – could reinstate them.

Once I had taken a number of cuttings (I took more than I needed in case they didn't all succeed), I decided that rather than pull out the old plants I would instead cut them down right to the ground, to just above any sign of green growth however small. After all I had nothing to lose – I planned to replace them all anyway. You have probably guessed the outcome – I found myself with an abundance of lavender plants because not only did the cuttings survive, so did the little seedlings I lifted and, not only that, the old plants flourished too, coming back thick and fast, compact and beautiful, and the flowers better than ever.

The natural world is great, and I adore how we humans believe we know it all when in actual fact we probably know very little. I love discovering things that are at odds with what I have believed to be the case. It is a huge confidence boost to the grower and gardener when something 'works' – it is empowering and makes us less afraid to just give it a go!

Had I adhered to the written information readily available to me, I would have been waiting several years for my lavender rows to be re-established. Instead, I felt I had triumphed, or my lavender had at least.

TIP: Lavender is a good deterrent to insects, so dried lavender in little bags hung in wardrobes and placed into clothes drawers can help repel clothes moths. Dried lavender scattered onto the floor of my chicken house keeps red mite at bay and I have discovered that the long, dried stalks, with the flowers removed, tied into little bundles, make the perfect fragrant firelighters.

IF YOU HAVE FIVE MINUTES

Late summer is a particularly nice time to be out and enjoying the garden. Here are a few small and simple jobs to do as you admire your space.

Courgettes

Harvest courgettes when they are small, sweet and tender. They will keep for 2 to 3 weeks wrapped in a damp towel in the base of the fridge (see table on page 59).

Houseplants

Pop houseplants outdoors, especially if rain is forecast. A shower will clean dust off the leaves and the fresh air will give them a welcome boost.

Spring Cabbages

Buy a packet of spring cabbage seeds or pick up a few plants if you see them in the garden centre. Late summer or early autumn is the perfect time to sow spring cabbage seeds – a must if you want to be able to get your hands on fresh greens in early spring when fresh veggies are expensive. Sow them in a seed tray or a small area of the garden – kept outside and watered, by next season they will be ready to prick out to a permanent bed. I lay an upturned metal hanging basket over my small seed bed once sown, to keep any birds off the tiny seedlings as they appear.

AUTUMN

EARLY AUTUMN

E ven though summer is officially over, early autumn is a beautiful season. Crops of sweetcorn, peppers, courgettes, cucumbers, aubergines, more tomatoes, early apples and pears, plus stone fruits, plums, greengages, blackcurrants, autumn raspberries and damsons will be ripening. The home grower will be harvesting relentlessly.

Some friends bemoan the downside of home growing, saying that after all that effort, everything is ready together and then is either wasted or given away. If you've ever had a similar thought, this chapter is for you. As much as I love to gift fruit and veggies to family and friends, I will – with my 'self-sufficiency' hat on – store or preserve the vast majority in one form or another.

Some produce can easily be dried in the microwave or in an oven or dehydrator if you have one but the hot sun is the best free energy to use. Other foods can be stored either by freezing, jamming, bottling, curing or pickling, enabling the joy of the home harvest season to continue all year long!

Save Sweet Pea Seeds

As early autumn approaches, you will notice that the plants will produce fewer flowers, and by the end of the month you will probably cut your last bunch, but all is not lost as we can continue cutting, only this time the harvest is for the seeds not the flowers.

As the leaves dry and begin to turn brown, you will also notice many flower pods forming. It is a good idea to reference the photo of your sweet peas that you took when they were at their best and then you can be reminded of the colours. My resplendent photo reminds me that the sweet peas have served me well. The plants are now beginning to look sparse and pale, and the scattering of remaining flowers will be drowned out and dominated by a collection of 2.5–5cm- (1–2 inch) long pea pods. They start off green then turn a creamy colour before eventually drying to a beige or brown.

The seed pods are ready to take from the plant when they feel hard and slightly brittle. Cut them from the plant, don't pull them (you could break the pod and lose the seeds or uproot the dying plant). I collect the pods into bowls – one for each colour – then break open the brittle pods and recover the large black seeds. As you collect the seeds, make a note of the colour, as all seeds look the same. Store them in paper bags (I use small envelopes), label them, then keep in a cool dark place along with your other seeds until late winter. If you don't mind a mix of colours in next year's planting, simply mark 'sweet peas, mixed'.

Plant Out Spring Cabbage Plants

Seeds sown last season (see page 186) will have germinated quickly in the warm conditions and can be pricked out and popped into their final growing position. The plants will be small, about 7.5–10cm (3–4 inches) tall and it is better to plant when the conditions are damp. These young plants will be very attractive to birds so protect them with netting until they become established.

It is incredible to believe that these small plants will make it all the way through the autumn winds and rain followed by winter frosts and snow. They will hardly move at all and you may think they are a lost cause. I have even had friends tell me their spring cabbages didn't do any good at all and they pulled them up... Don't do that! These beauties will excel all by themselves. As the days get a bit longer and the sun that bit warmer in early spring, these little cabbages will blossom into prize specimens at a time when fresh crops to be enjoyed are in short supply and expensive.

Make Way for Winter Staples

I rely on these crops to get me through the winter months, so it is important to make sure they are in the best of health. Clear away any fallen or rotting leaves from the base of the plants that could cause problems by harbouring disease or slugs and snails. The leaves can be popped into the compost bin.

Tall kale varieties, sprouts and broccoli will benefit from a support to protect them from strong winds. A tall cane inserted into the ground alongside the plant then tied with compostable string will give good protection. I can't tell you how many times I have had a prize-looking sprout plant, only to find it lying flat on the ground following a storm or high winds. Once they have fallen over, they don't seem to want to stand up again – I end up having to harvest soil-splattered sprouts at ground level.

Inspect your leeks regularly and, if you see any sign of one of them throwing out a seed pod, harvest that leek and use it straight away. Left to bolt or 'go to seed', the stalk with the seed pod will grow tall and thick and develop a flower and the leek will be a thick stem and not really suitable for eating – not poisonous in any way, just tough. I would still use it, however, perhaps cut up in a stew or soup.

Why do some vegetables go to seed? It is a strange one, because there may be one onion, one beetroot, one leek, or one cauliflower that does this yet the rest of the row will remain intact. I have read that it is due to the plant being too hot, too cold, too dry, the soil too rich, etc, yet if that were the case why isn't the whole row affected? I am still unsure why it happens, but what I do know is that I will harvest that specimen first, eat it, then forget it ever happened!

The Luffa Gourd Challenge

My two large green luffas having reached their potential needed now to dry out if I am to be able to transform them into useable natural pan scourers and cleaning aids. The days are shorter, the sun not so strong and after a cold night of just 5°C (40°F), I wondered whether the greenhouse was going to be the best place.

Further online research revealed there were growers who had completed the drying process in a low oven. Some had cut their luffas into large pieces to dry and some left them whole. This really is a learning process so I decided to cut one into 15 cm (6 inch) pieces and leave the other one whole. I popped them into a low oven at just 80-100°C (Gas Mark ¼/ 200°F) for an hour and very quickly the skins turned from a sage green to pale brown but the Luffas were feeling soft and squidgy. My gut instinct was to slow this drying down – this was happening far too fast.

I feared for the fruits. The skin on the outside felt hard to the touch yet the whole fruit felt soft and squidgy when squeezed. I slit each skin with a sharp blade to release any liquid which might otherwise, if left with no escape, cause rot. It was no surprise when a watery liquid dripped from the fruits so I hung them outside for a day to allow this excess moisture to escape.

I then took the Luffas, slotted a length of string through the very thick skin and left them in the warm, dry airing cupboard for three full weeks.

I made a note to resist the oven for drying luffas. Next time I will slit the skins and simply hang in a warm, dry place until completely dried and until I can hear the seeds rattle.

SWEET SWEETCORN

Your sweetcorn should now be ready to harvest. This is an exciting time – each plant can yield three large cobs and you know they're ready to harvest when you see the silks at the tip of the cob turn from silky smooth, blond ponytails to a messy hairdo resembling mid-brown dried frizz.

Take the biggest cob, usually this is the one at the base of the plant, and – just like broad beans (see page 140) – pull downwards on the cob in a swift, sharp movement (not upwards because then you are in danger of uprooting the plant).

Peel back the tight green covering of leaves to reveal the ripe, deep-yellow corn inside. The browned silks under the leaves (one actually belongs to each tiny piece of corn) can easily be rubbed off if you're wearing a rubber glove. This is a real example, just like potatoes, where supermarket or shop-bought specimens cannot possibly compete with the freshness of home-grown.

So many recipes offer various preparations and flavour enhancements for sweetcorn – they can be boiled, barbecued, roasted and steamed, but for me the absolutely perfect way to serve them is by harvesting them just before I need them – within the hour if I can, to capture every morsel of freshness and then . . .

No need to remove leaves or silks, to cook simply pop the whole cob, leaves and all, into the microwave for 4 minutes on high power (6 minutes for 2 cobs) – and that is it! Minimum energy usage, nutrients captured within those tight leaves and no washing up.

Holding the hot cob firmly with a tea towel or oven glove, chop off the stalk end of the cob with a sharp knife. Then simply peel off the leaves to reveal the steaming hot bright yellow corn below. 'Him Indoors' likes his with lashings of butter; for me I enjoy them just as they are, with nothing added.

'AT LAST' AUBERGINES!

Pot-grown aubergines can be harvested now. Unlike some other vegetables, I have found that biggest is not always best with aubergines: I once grew an enormous aubergine – it was as big as my face! I was nurturing it and boasting about its size and stature, but found that I had left it far too long. The skin had turned pale and dull and was tough. When squeezed, my fingers left an indentation in the fruit and, when cut, the flesh inside was turning brown, tasted bitter and had formed large seeds. It was still edible – I used every morsel – but I learned to harvest them when the fruits are ever so slightly under-ripe and haven't yet formed seeds.

For me, the perfect fruit should be dark and shiny and, when squeezed lightly, should feel spongey, with any slight indentation from the finger squeeze readily bouncing back.

A fine size is 15–20cm (6–8 inches) long and about 7.5cm (3 inches) wide at the base. I cut mine with scissors or secateurs. Beware the prickly green calyx attached to the fruit – it has nasty thorns! Use gloves if necessary and cut the stalk above – keep the calyx attached as the aubergine will last for longer.

Home-grown peppers, aubergines and chillies probably won't all ripen at once, which is good – cut them from the plants as

needed. Unlike their perfectly formed, coloured, sprayed and plastic-packaged supermarket equivalents, home-grown fruit will be different shapes and sizes, with a few knobbly bits, yet will carry a depth of flavour you've probably never come across before.

SWEET PEPPERS AND CHILLIES

Each plant will now be tall and bushy, and the peppers and chillies as they ripen will come alive! Each pepper plant can produce between 6 and 8 super fruits. A good year will yield many colourful gorgeous peppers. One or two chilli plants will keep you well stocked for the year as they will be festooned with bright fruits.

Peppers start off green then, as they mature and ripen, they will change colour – some to red and some to yellow, depending on the variety. However, I have known some green peppers refuse to change colour even though its neighbour on the same plant is looking red. I like a basket of traffic-light colours so all of this is absolutely fine and the slight bitterness from green peppers suits some salads and dishes more than the sweeter red fruits. Chilli plants too will replace the white flowers with tiny green fruits, turning then to flame-bright red or can be harvested green (we have all seen the mixed bags in the supermarkets).

Once harvested, chillies and peppers will last up to two weeks in the fridge but I like to have a winter supply as they are great for cooking and can be used from frozen. To harvest, use a pair of secateurs to neatly cut the fruit from the main plant. The stalk is very thick so don't be tempted to pull at it. I like to retain a decent section of stalk with the fruit so that the pepper can enjoy a longer shelf-life once harvested.

Small fresh peppers and chillies can be frozen just as they are without the need to blanch, then sliced from frozen and used in cooking. Larger fruits are better sliced and then they are ready to use as required. I slice them, lay them on trays, pop the trays into the freezer then – once firm – transfer them into freezer bags or boxes. That's it – no fuss or faff.

I can never have too many peppers. Believe me, they make the perfect tasty soup throughout the year, can be added to pasta sauces, casseroles, curries etc.

Red Pepper Soup

I use my frozen peppers during the winter months to make this easy, quick and warming soup. It freezes well too and – by the way – it is okay to freeze the soup even though frozen peppers were used to make it. Anything taken from the freezer that goes on to be cooked can then be frozen again.

Serves 6

YOU WILL NEED
medium saucepan
chopping board
vegetable knife
hand blender

1 tbsp oil (I used rapeseed but any oil of choice will do)
1 onion, roughly chopped
50g (1¾oz) chorizo or bacon (optional)
2 garlic cloves, chopped, or 1 tsp garlic granules
1 mild chilli, sliced and discard the seeds and core (fresh or
    frozen)
2 or 3 red peppers, deseeded and sliced or cut into chunks
    (when using frozen I consider a handful to be about half a
    pepper – so 4–6 frozen handfuls)
500ml (17fl oz) vegetable stock (home-made or stock cube)
1 tbsp balsamic or malt vinegar
½ tsp salt

Heat the oil in a medium saucepan over a low heat, then add
the chopped onion and the chorizo or bacon (if using). Fry
for 10 minutes until the onion is just softening and the chorizo
sizzling or bacon colouring brown. Add the garlic or granules,
chilli and the peppers and stir regularly over a high heat for
5 minutes until the peppers begin to tinge with golden brown
at the edges. Add the stock, vinegar and salt, stir well, then
bring to the boil. Once boiling, reduce the heat to a steady
simmer, cover partially with a lid and cook for 15–20 minutes
until the peppers are quite tender. Remove from the heat.

Blitz with a hand blender until smooth. Taste and check the seasoning, adding more salt if required.

'Jar of Fire' Chilli Sauce

If you have grown a very hot chilli pepper plant in a pot – and there are several varieties to choose from – it is my guess you have far too many fruits. Even if you ate chillies every day, you'll struggle to get through them all before next harvest!

I often grow a very hot bird's-eye or scotch bonnet chilli. Just one plant will become covered in ripe small (very hot) bright red fruits that looks so beautiful and even though I have a greenhouse, I bring mine into the house because it can look so stunning – almost like a well-decorated Christmas tree.

I continue to enjoy the decorative plant until every chilli is bright red then I clip off every one with scissors and either freeze, dry or make into the hottest, most flavoursome chilli sauce. One Christmas I popped this into small jars and included it as a hamper item for family and it went down a treat. Not one for the faint hearted!

Makes about 700g (1lb 9oz)

YOU WILL NEED
food processor
large saucepan
hand blender or liquidiser
small glass jars with screw-top lids – I save my smallest glass
    jars for this, 100-150g (3½–5½ oz) size
large casserole pan with a lid

tea towel or cloth

2 onions, peeled
100g (3½oz) bird's-eye chillies (or chillies of your choice, the
 heat will depend on the variety you use)
1 large red pepper, deseeded
2 garlic cloves, peeled
2 tbsp rapeseed oil or olive oil
2 tbsp sugar
1 tsp salt
6 fresh ripe tomatoes, quartered
150ml (5fl oz) malt vinegar
250ml (8fl oz) apple juice

Blitz the onion, chillies (as they are – no need to remove seeds, etc.), red pepper and garlic to a rough pulp in a food processor.

Heat the oil in the large saucepan over a medium heat, add the chopped chilli mix and fry for 10 minutes until softened. Add the sugar, salt, quartered tomatoes, vinegar and apple juice and simmer uncovered for 20 minutes. Remove from the heat and allow to cool slightly, then blitz to a smooth sauce with a hand blender or liquidiser.

Sterilise the jars according to the method on page 150. Fill the jars, screw on the lids and then to preserve the sauce, stand each jar in a large saucepan, lay a small tea towel or cloth in your largest casserole dish or stock pan then set the sealed jars onto the cloth, tucking the cloth between each glass jar so that they don't touch

each other and bang together. Cover the whole lot in cold water and make sure the water covers the jars. Bring to the boil for 10 minutes then turn off the heat, cover and leave for 40 minutes. After this time remove the jars when cool enough to handle. This final process forms a seal inside the jar which will ensure the sauce stays fresh for up to a year. Once opened I keep in the fridge for up to 6 weeks.

If the sauce is not going to be used regularly, bottle it in even smaller jars then there will be minimal waste if an opened jar is not used up.

DRYING STONE FRUITS

Stone fruits dry incredibly well. I have dried apricots and plums and they lasted right up until the following spring. It's so easy to do. Mother Nature has provided apricots, plums, greengages and damsons all with a cutting line down one side. I am sure this is no accident and it's there for us as a guide, so that we know exactly where to place our knife.

Run a knife down this line, twist the two halves of the fruit in opposite directions and it will come apart. Remove the stone, then either place the halves cut side up in a single layer in a dehydrator or lay on cooling racks and place in a gently warm oven 80-100°C (Gas Mark ¼/200°F). The drying may take 2–3 hours in the oven but more than one tray (I tend to have three trays in the oven at a time) can be drying at the same time. The fruits are completely dried once they feel non-sticky. Not even the slightest bit of stickiness should be present, otherwise they will turn mouldy once stored. Dried plums are beautiful and very dark once dried. Dried apricots turn a pale brown, not the bright yellow/orange of many of the bought ones (those vibrant shop-bought ones will have been dried and preserved using sulphur dioxide), yet your home dried darker ones still keep incredibly well and right through the winter.

PLUM TART

This recipe is always on the menu in early autumn and takes your freshly picked fruits to another level. Super tasty, looks professional and a great option for those not wanting to make pastry along with the necessary rolling out and baking blind – this is super quick. Use plums or any fresh and, even better, slightly under-ripe stone fruits (apricots, nectarines, peaches, greengages). This is a cross between a cake and a tart though easier to make than either of the two!

Serves 8–10

YOU WILL NEED
23cm (9 inch) loose-bottomed fluted flan tin
small jug
zester or microplane
large mixing bowl
hand held electric whisk
small angled palette knife (optional)
cooling rack
pastry brush

zest of 1 lemon and 2 tsp juice

30ml (1fl oz) whole milk

125g (4¼oz) margarine or softened butter, plus a little extra
    for greasing

125g (4¼oz) caster sugar

1 egg

125g (4¼oz) ground almonds or 50/50 ground almonds and
    ground rice

125g (4¼oz) plain flour (or gluten-free flour/rice flour for a
    gluten-free tart)

10–12 Victoria plums (about 500g/1lb 2oz)

    (4–5 slightly under-ripe peaches and nectarines work well
    too)

2–3 heaped tbsp apricot jam, to glaze

Grease the tin.

Grate the zest of the lemon into a roomy mixing bowl, then
halve and squeeze the 2 teaspoons of juice into a small jug,
add the milk and set aside to thicken.

Add the margarine or butter and the sugar to the bowl with
the zest and cream together using the hand held whisk until
light and fluffy. Add the egg and whisk well, then fold in the
ground almonds or ground rice/ground almond mixture and
flour, then finally the thickened milk. Mix until everything is
well combined. The mixture will be quite thick.

Transfer the mixture to the prepared tin and smooth it
out using a small angled palette knife or the back of a
teaspoon. Spread out to the edges then firm down until very
smooth. Use the tip of a teaspoon to mould the mix into
every contour at the edge of the tin. Take your time because
this will make all the difference to your finished tart. Once
completely smooth and flawless, pop the tin into the freezer

for 15–20 minutes to firm up while you prepare the plums or other fruits.

Preheat the oven to 160°C (Gas Mark 3/325°F). Slice the fruits in half lengthways, remove the stone then slice each half into four slices, lengthways. Each fruit will yield 8 slices. Under-ripe fruits are just that bit easier to handle, being more firm and less juicy than very ripe ready-to-eat ones.

Take the tart tin from the freezer. The base will now be quite firm which makes it super easy to decorate the surface. Here you can let loose your artistic flair! The plums need to fit side by side, nice and snug and quite tight, with just the slightest overlap. Start around the outside edge then place a second row inside and a final few slices of fruit to fill the centre space. Transfer to the oven and bake for 1 hour. The fruits will have softened but will still have retained their shape and the base will be firm to the touch. As it has baked at such a low temperature, it will be only very slightly browned.

Remove from the oven and leave to cool to room temperature on a cooling rack. When the tart has cooled, heat the apricot jam in a small saucepan with 1–2 tablespoons of water to loosen it. The jam needs to be a thick consistency but thin enough to be able to brush over the fruits. Brush carefully over the top – the jam will not only glaze but also add a thin layer of sweetness.

Serve at room temperature with cream or ice cream.

HARVESTING APPLES

Autumn really is harvest time and, over the coming weeks, apples and pears will be in abundance. There are so many varieties of apple to choose from and many older houses with gardens will have an old knobbly apple tree in a corner that seems to have been there forever. An apple tree can live for forty-five years or so!

Apart from the 'July drop' – a natural process (and one helped along by me, see page 143) where the apple tree will discard weaker fruits to make way for stronger ones – you will start to notice a few windfalls this season, especially following strong winds. In some ways these fallen fruits are the most exciting. They are the first apples of the season and who doesn't love apple pie?

Many people will give away apples and pears to willing takers, though they can also be successfully stored and preserved.

Storing Apples

I grow lots of apples and they store exceptionally well. I invested in an apple store some years ago – it's a chest of drawers, in essence, but each drawer is slatted to provide good ventilation. The apples are laid in the drawers, ensuring they are not touching each other, and kept in the cool dark garage. Any well-ventilated cool place is perfect and for those without an apple store the fruits can be wrapped individually in newspaper and stored until required on trays in a garage, cellar or any other cool, dark frost free place.

TIP: An apple store is the perfect place to cure potatoes too, before the apple season arrives
(see page 145).

I check my apples monthly and discard any perished fruits or use any that are showing the first signs of rot or damage: I cut off any bruises or blemishes and use the undamaged part of the fruits. My home-grown, non-sprayed apples will keep me supplied with apples in the kitchen right up until the next spring. Apples are around 80 per cent water, so as they gradually dry out they become softer and much sweeter and my later apples need no added sugar whatsoever in baking.

On the subject of the nutritional value of stored fruit and veggies, I have often been asked and wondered myself whether nutrients are lost during storage. I have discussed this on page 59 but to sum up – freshly harvested contain a rich mix of vitamins and while some diminish during storage others increase as produce matures and sweetens.

I have read that apples bought in the supermarket can be up to one year old. In a warehouse setting they often sit for at least 9–12 months and one investigation showed that on average apples on the supermarket shelves are 14 months old. I have no doubt this is the case: for example, I bought a pack of Granny Smith apples in May that had been grown in France so it is obvious to me (as the seasons in France are very similar to those in the UK) that those apples were grown the previous year. It would not be possible to grow and harvest an apple by late spring of the same year.

Having acquired a better understanding of seasonality, how far food has had to travel, how long it must have had to be washed, sprayed, treated and stored in order to keep it looking as fresh as the day it was picked, I am even more convinced that even the smallest home-grown harvest can make all the difference. If I have grown food myself I will also do my very best to look after it and use up every morsel.

I bought all the apple processing kit a few years ago – well when I say 'all the kit,' I am referring to a home apple crusher and fruit press. It is only a small affair, but I can make almost enough fruit juice to keep me going through the winter. I don't do it in a sophisticated way – I wash then crush my apples and pears, push them through the press and decant the pink-tinged juice into plastic bottles that I have kept back from supermarket-bought orange juice, then pop them into the freezer. If you are wondering, 'how big is your freezer?' – yes, I have had to invest in an additional freezer in the garage. This one is dedicated to preserving my home-grown produce: there is something so feel-good about eating home-produced food that hasn't been messed about with. I'm sure this is not for everyone, and I accept I am becoming a bit obsessive in my old age, but it is now something of a way of life for me. When my granddaughter visits she always asks for a glass of my 'epic' apple juice!

Dried Apple Slices

I am a real fan of dried home-grown fruits. I use them in many baking and cooking recipes and eat them as a snack and – knowing they have been harvested from my own trees, have not been sprayed to preserve the fruit, kill bugs or to treat or prevent disease – I am more than happy to dry the skins too. If you see an apple in the fruit bowl looking a bit soft and wrinkled this is an excellent way to make use of it.

Apples, pears, plums and apricots can be dried in the oven, in the sun or in a dehydrator. When we get a super-hot sunny day I will often start my apples off outside in the sunshine and then finish them off in the oven. I have a small dehydrator, but for apples I can fit more slices in on several racks in one go in the oven.

YOU WILL NEED
mixing bowl
sharp knife
chopping board
apple corer (optional)
cooling racks

dessert apples, washed
2 tsp citric acid (as a green cleaner I always have this on the shelf!) or 8 tsp lemon juice or white vinegar

Wash the fruits then prepare the bowl of acidified water. This will prevent the apple slices (or any fruits) from turning brown, and will destroy any bacteria. If you don't have citric acid, lemon juice or vinegar can be used, though you will need four times the amount. Add the citric acid (or lemon juice/vinegar) to a bowl then pour over about 50ml (1¾fl oz) hot water and stir until dissolved. Once the solution is clear, top up with cold water to make 1 litre (34fl oz). If using lemon juice or vinegar, simply add to a bowl then top up with cold water to 1 litre (34fl oz).

The whole of the apple is edible, and each element contains a unique set of nutrients, even the stalk. However, a dried stalk and the seeds may not be the most appetising and it is not advisable to eat lots of the seeds as they contain traces of cyanide, so I remove them.

Twist and remove the stalk and remove the core if you wish (though I quite like to see a dried apple slice with the core intact). Using a sharp knife, cut the apple into thin slices about the thickness of a £1 coin (about 3-4mm), starting at the stalk end. There are gadgets available that will do this quickly and neatly for you, such as a mandoline, but I do it by hand. Once cut, plunge the slices into the acidic water immediately. Leave the slices in the water for 5 minutes.

Take the slices from the water and spread them out in a single layer on cooling racks. I put the racks outside for an hour or two when the weather is warm, even hot with a gentle breeze. The excess moisture soon evaporates from the slices. Turn them once while they dry out. If you think you may be troubled by flying bugs, a thin piece of muslin cloth or netting can be suspended over the racks. Most insects, however, will not trouble your drying slices, as they are not attracted by the smell of citrus.

Once the excess moisture has evaporated from your fruits, they can be finished off in the oven or dehydrator for 6–8 hours if the sun is no longer shining. The oven temperature needs to be a very low 80-100°C (Gas Mark ¼/200°F), or lower if you can. It is important that the apple slices dry rather than bake and change colour. The drying time will vary depending on the thickness of the slices.

The finished dried apple slice should feel leathery to the touch and still soft and pliable, but not sticky or wet at all. Once completely dried, store in airtight jars in a cool place. They will last for at least 6 months or until you've eaten them. Dry them for longer and you have apple crisps which are also delicious.

CITRUS CRUMB

Grapefruit, orange, lemon and lime skins can be dried in the sun until crisp then blitzed to make the most gorgeous citrus crumb. One large grapefruit and two orange skins filled a 450g (1lb) glass jar and I use the vibrant bright orange crumb regularly in baking, cooking, salad dressings, in fruit bread, sprinkled over ice cream and over yoghurt at breakfast – I love it! In fact – use in any recipe that calls for citrus zest – about 1 tbsp dried zest will be the equivalent of the fresh zest from 1 lemon. Free food and no waste!

YOU WILL NEED
peeler
sharp knife
chopping board
cooling rack
dehydrator or low oven (optional)
liquidizer or food processor
clean glass jar with a lid

washed peel from any citrus fruits

Slice the peels into strips about 1cm (½ inch) thick – don't worry about the bitter pith. Pith is edible and dries to such a thin layer that the bitterness is lost and, once blitzed, you'll not detect it. Lay the cut pieces onto a cooling rack then leave out in the sun: I like to make the most of a sunny day and Mother Nature's free energy. Flies hate the smell of citrus (they don't bother my peels at all when they are drying), but you can cover with a net if you like. The peels are sufficiently dried when they snap easily.

The peels can be also dried in a low conventional oven 80-100°C (Gas Mark ¼/200°F) or dehydrator. It will take several hours for them to dry completely.

Blitz the dried peels to a fine crumb in the liquidizer or food processor then store in a glass jar with a lid. The citrus blast given off when the lid is unscrewed is wonderful!

GRANOLA

One of my favourite recipes, which makes excellent use of my home-dried fruits, is this easy granola. Have you seen how much additional refined sugar they add to some of the packets in the shops? It is easy to remember – 100g of nearly everything!

Makes about 1kg (2lb 4oz)

YOU WILL NEED
scissors
large mixing bowl
spoon
large baking tray
reusable baking parchment liner
clean jar for storage

300g (10½oz) porridge oats

1 tsp each of salt and ground spice (cinnamon, nutmeg or mixed spice)

100g (3½oz) unsalted nuts (any combo, chopped)

grated zest of 1 lemon or orange (or use 1 tbsp Citrus Crumb – see page 210)

100g (3½oz) nuts and/or seeds (any mix)

100g (3½oz) coconut flakes or desiccated coconut

100ml (3½fl oz) oil (sunflower, vegetable or coconut, or oil of choice)

100ml (3½fl oz) syrup (maple, golden syrup or honey)

100g (3½oz) dried fruits (I use any combination of my home-dried fruits, including dried apple slices finely diced with scissors)

Preheat the oven to 200°C (Gas Mark 6/400°F) and line a large baking tray with reusable baking parchment.

Mix together all the ingredients, except the dried fruits, in a large mixing bowl. I start with the oats, salt, spice, nuts and seeds, citrus zest, seeds and coconut and mix them together well, then drizzle over the oil and whichever syrup you decide to use. Stir well – the mix will clump up but that's perfect.

Spread out the clumped-up mixture on the lined large baking tray and bake in the oven for 20 minutes. After 10 minutes, take the tray from the oven and stir the mix around with a fork. After the full 20 minutes, the granola will be lightly toasted and just beginning to colour. Using the baking parchment liner as an aid, lift and slide the mix back into the bowl and stir through the dried fruits. Once cool, store in an airtight jar. The granola will keep up to 6 weeks in a jar, though it has never been put to the test for any longer, as it is soon eaten up.

MID AUTUMN

Berry colours, warm days and colder nights. Much of the harvest is in, prepped and stored as jars of jam, chutney and pickle, dried fruit and herbs; the freezer is stocked with frozen berries, apple juice, elderflower syrup, peppers and chillies; and I have fresh greens in the garden to keep me going through the winter months with garlic, onions and roots in the garage.

The trees and hedgerows take on their autumn glow as the leaves change, the rosehips emerge, shiny conkers are ripe for foraging and transforming into free laundry detergent, rosehips shine red and bejewelled on misty days and the sultry dark purple sloe berry hugging the thorny branches of the blackthorn tree is ready to harvest. While it may be considered that the growing for the year is finished there are still some surprise plantings that can be done.

Clearing and Tidying

The greenhouse and the plants inside will be slowing down. After collecting the harvest from pepper, basil and tomato plants, the plants can be removed from the soil and composted. The spent compost too provides a 'dry' layer to the 'wet' from the discarded plant. Tall sweetcorn plants can be pulled up and composted too, but bear in mind that the stems are thick,

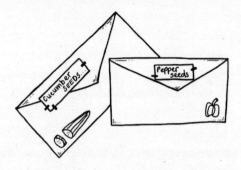

up to 5cm (2 inches) in places, so after lifting I lay the spent plant along the ground and chop the stem into rough 20cm (8 inch) 'bite-size' chunks with a spade before transferring them to the compost.

Harvest the large overgrown dried and drying pods on tall runner and climbing bean plants as they will be your next year's free seeds. Some pods will be completely dry and brittle whereas others may need a little longer. If the weather is turning wet and windy, it won't be long before a hearty gust blows the plants over so get in there before Mother Nature to ensure next year's seeds are saved. Harvest the pods and store them somewhere dry in a single layer until the shells are completely dried and brittle and the bean seeds easily pop out. In weeks to come, I can quickly shell next year's seeds, label and store in paper bags or envelopes over winter. There is also a free food opportunity here – see page 231.

Even though it is a fairly time-consuming job as I clear the pots, veggie plot and greenhouse, I take my time to remove metal ties, strings, canes and plant labels. They can all be reused next year. Plastic and wooden plant labels can be cleaned quickly in soapy water and any stubborn pencil removed with a damp cloth dipped in dry bicarbonate of soda. Sweep the greenhouse clean and generally tidy it up, and be ready to bring in any plants that need to be kept free from frost.

I have two lemon trees in pots and, once the greenhouse is emptied of tomato plants, cucumbers and the like, in come the citrus trees. In some warmer climates, and in their native habitats, plants that here in the UK are considered annuals (lasting only one season) will grow year after year. It is possible to overwinter tomatoes, peppers, aubergines and chilli plants by simply cutting them back so they grow and fruit again the following year but, sadly, here in the UK, once temperatures drop (and especially once the frost hits) they generally succumb to the elements.

Take a Five-minute Tour

This is purely an observation but it helps me to have a regular five-minute tour of the veg and fruit garden, pulling out a weed or two as I go.

My rows of kale look good – they resist insect damage. The sprouts, I had noted on a previous check, had been badly attacked by caterpillars and I had considered pulling them up but decided (so I thought) that the damage was done so I would leave them. The leaves were lacy, the plants I thought would be weakened and there'd be little chance of a good crop.

However, much to my delight, they were beginning to replenish themselves. New, bright luscious leaves were emerging from the crown, the damaged and eaten leaves were lower down the stalk and the button sprouts growing below were flawless. I had thought the caterpillars may have damaged

this crop but no. The caterpillars have had their season, they will do no more damage now because the summer has passed and the sprouts – seemingly because they are healthy and strong – were able to resist a nibble or two. Another example of leaving things alone – no spraying needed. Nature can sort the job out with a little patience.

Look Ahead to Next Year

The growing season has finished, trees and bushes after dropping their leaves will go to sleep for the winter (known as their dormant stage) and there may be few gardening jobs to do, though now is the perfect time to think about your plans for next year.

Take a look at your garden and decide whether there is anything you want to change ahead of next year; maybe extend a veggie bed, add a shed or greenhouse. All of these things are better jotted down, planned and actually done over the winter period so that you are good to go in the spring. Planning a new bed, for example can be marked out, any turf or roots removed and then prepped over winter. A good layer of compost spread in autumn will ensure the soil is in perfect condition for sowing and planting the following spring.

Prune your Apple and Pear Trees

The varying instructions about when to prune often leave me confused, though I have found that a good time is soon after leaves have fallen and before the weather has turned really cold and any wintering insects or small animals have hibernated. My rule is to take a look at the tree or fruit bush and imagine it needs to be the shape of a wine glass. There will be books that advise 'this' or 'that' but my rule is the tree or bush needs to be accessible and not too high so that the fruit can be reached, the branches not too crowded or crossing each other and any weak or dying parts need to be removed. I used to be afraid of pruning, but now stick to these few general rules. I believe it is better done when the plant is asleep, not bearing flowers or fruit or leaves. The weather needs to be cold though not frosty and, if in doubt about how much to cut off, reduce a branch by no more than one third – more can always be taken off in early spring as growth restarts. Remember to wipe down loppers or secateurs with surgical spirit when moving from plant to plant, to avoid spreading disease (see page 19).

Check your Pots

The pots that have done you proud over the summer, whether for flowers, fruits or veggies, may be looking tired and forlorn as foliage begins to die off. Mint and chives may look finished for the year though I have found it is still not too late for a late haircut. I usually trim only half of the plant, so that I still have a few fresh leaves to call on when needed. The other half is cut right back. If there is an early frost, there may be no further growth, yet if the autumn is mild and warm there will be an enjoyable final fresh harvest of bright young leaves.

Plant Spring Flowering Bulbs

Bulbs that have been kept in storage after splitting to separate and drying back in summer can now be planted outside into the ground or in pots while the soil is still warm. Fill pots three-quarters full with compost then add a layer of bulbs. I like to pack them in to ensure an abundance of colour in spring. Top off with another layer of compost then leave pots outside. Mother Nature will do the watering.

Bulbs planted in small upcycled containers, painted plant pots or decorative boxes, etc. can be planted up either this month or next month. They make excellent Christmas gifts and I keep mine in the greenhouse. I refrain from watering until a month before Christmas to ensure growth doesn't start too early.

Rake Leaves for Storage

Autumn leaves will have started to fall and on a chilly 'still' autumn day I quite enjoy raking the colourful specimens into small piles all over the garden. I then follow up with a wheelbarrow and use two pieces of thick cardboard to sandwich them together and transfer each pile into the barrow.

This simple 'board' method is much more effective than trying to lift leaves from the ground by hand. Just when I think I have a decent clutch of leaves by the time I have my hands around them, lifted them up then transferred to a wheelbarrow so many make an escape, leaving a trail on the ground. It's great fun for children but not when you want to get the job done. A clutch between two boards plus a 'still' day will be much less labour intensive.

Have you thought about a leaf store? Many people I know fill plastic bags with leaves and take them to the local refuse tip! I have to confess there was a time I used to do this too. However, they are a fantastic natural, free, delicious compost material – not as rich in nutrients as a full garden compost, but still a brilliant top dressing for any plant, a compost for starting off seeds, a brilliant mulch to suppress weeds and retain moisture. Again, it's FREE. Make drainage holes in a plastic bag (an old compost bag is a perfect recycle item), add the leaves, water them, tie the bag and leave it in an out-of-the-way place. Better still, if you have space, construct a wire leaf store. It's similar to a compost bin but, rather than a wooden construction, it's made of wire. I think this is better as air can flow freely and there is much less weight, so it doesn't need to be as robust. Plus, being constructed of wire ensures the leaves don't escape. Water it if the leaves are dry, cover with an old piece of carpet to keep the heat in and in around 18 months you will be carving out a dark crumbly worm-filled loam which is perfect for your garden.

BUY AND PLANT AUTUMN ONIONS, GARLIC AND SHALLOTS

Planted between now and early winter, either into the ground or in outside pots, these tough alliums need very little care and will be ready to harvest in early summer (rather than late summer as for spring-planted varieties). This is perfect for those with limited space as their spot can then be offered to other crops after harvest. The green spikes soon seem to show through, there are no weeds competing for space, and it is great to have something to inspect when having a walk through the garden even on the most challenging weather days.

Garlic, onions and shallots planted now will be ready to harvest in early/midsummer, or when the bulbs have grown and the green tops have turned yellow. Unlike spring-sown varieties that will occupy their bed for much longer, these crops will be ready, lifted and drying and creating space for a follow-on crop – maybe sweetcorn (see page 298).

For all onions and garlic grown from sets (the name given to immature onion bulbs for planting), I plant them 10cm (4 inches) apart in rows about 23cm (9 inches) apart and at a depth where the tip is barely visible on the surface of the ground. You can also follow the instructions on the packet.

I have also had success with onions in pots! They are easy to grow and don't need a lot of room, and are a great starter crop, but bear in mind too that onions are not expensive to buy, so if you are wanting to grow something more exciting that you can't get in the shops, save your space for a different crop. Try elephant garlic, for example: it's huge fun and yields a large garlic bulb the following summer which is milder in taste than the garlic we buy in the shops. It's a great one for showing off to your friends too, and makes an amazing edible gift idea.

MY FAVOURITE WINTER VARIETIES:

Garlic – Garlic Germidour (Purple Wight)
White onion – Autumn Champion
Red onion – Electric
Banana shallot – Griselle
Elephant garlic – often referred to as Great-Headed Garlic

SLOE GIN

I make a bottle of sloe gin most years and like to decant it into miniature bottles and gift it at Christmas time, adding it to a homemade hamper of edible goodies. It's expensive to buy, yet very simple to make, and the longer you keep it, the better it tastes. If you want your sloe gin for Christmas, start making it as soon as you see the purple berries in the hedge-rows that are just soft to the touch. Be careful though – the branches have sharp thorns!

Sloe gin made at home from just sloe berries, sugar and gin is a beautiful dark red, almost purple liqueur. It makes stunning cocktails, can be enjoyed as an aperitif, and I have also used it in my cooking and baking.

Do not be tempted to think that the cheapest gin will turn itself into the finest sloe gin. The first time I made it I did just that. The next time I used a good-quality gin and the difference was quite remarkable. And use ripe berries: they need to feel soft between the fingers, not hard and bullet-like. If they are hard, they are not ripe.

Makes 1 litre (34fl oz)

YOU WILL NEED
needle
1-litre (34fl oz) bottle with a screw cap (I use a 1-litre gin
    bottle still half full of gin)
funnel
muslin cloth

200g (7oz) ripe sloe berries, washed if you like
500ml (17fl oz) gin
120g (4¼oz) caster sugar

Prick each berry with a needle to pierce the skin, then drop it into the bottle containing the gin. Alternatively, freeze the berries then the skins will split of their own accord.

Add the sugar to the bottle, screw on the top, give everything a good shake, then leave in a cool place, laid on its side and away from sunlight, but somewhere handy because you need to shake it every day until all the sugar has dissolved. The sugar should dissolve after about a week. After that you need to shake it every week up to Christmas! I do it on Fridays, so that I remember.

When the festive season is upon us and you are ready to enjoy or gift the gin, simply strain the berries from your gin using a muslin cloth secured in a funnel and transfer to either a decanter or clean bottle (or bottles) for gifts.

SEASONAL SPECIAL – MAKE AN INSECT HOTEL

I never used to give a thought to the over-wintering of insects until I became more environmentally conscious. As well as us humans, plants and animals, insects need to be able to protect themselves from the worst that the winter weather will bring.

On a visit to a garden centre, I was enchanted by a row of insect hotels – or bug hotels as they are often called – I loved them. I initially thought 'great idea but not a great price'! Some sell for huge sums. I decided instead to have a go at making one myself.

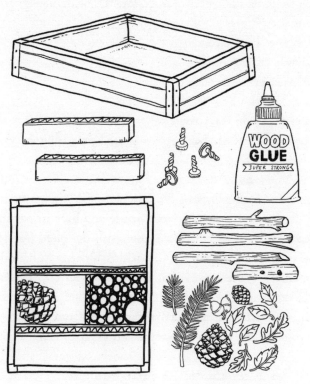

It's a great idea for children too – as soon as my grand-daughter saw it she said, 'Will you help me to make one, Granny?' She went off to forage for the insect bedding as I began to refashion a wooden box. One of the greatest pleasures for me is the engagement of children in our natural world, as they begin to understand that we are part of nature and that nature shouldn't be trying to fit around us.

YOU WILL NEED

a minimum 30cm (12 inch) wooden box (or make your own
    with wood offcuts if you're handy with a saw and screws)
stiff cardboard or pieces of wood for creating partitions
glue
pinecones (for ladybirds)
bamboo canes (for bees)
dried leaves (for beetles)
cardboard (for lacewings)
twigs and sticks (for spiders)
a square of chicken wire stapled over to keep the furnishings
    in place.

Make holes in the back of the box so that it can be mounted with screws into the wall. Next, create and glue in partitions for each of the materials used, these can be made from thin wood or sturdy cardboard. The box depth needs to be around 10-15cm (4-6 inches) so that the insects can crawl right to the back for the best shelter. When the glue is dry, fill the rooms with the different materials, cover the front with chicken wire to keep everything in place and find a good spot for your hotel.

The home for the insects needs to be sheltered and as

waterproof as possible, so let your imagination run wild! I covered the roof of mine with small twigs to resemble rough thatching and positioned it in a sheltered corner out of direct wind and rain. If the cones get wet they will close up – so a nice dry spot is the most comfy.

LATE AUTUMN

The summer's residual warmth diminishes and there is a nip in the air by morning and evening. I try not to be sad that the early autumn colours and golden glow are fading. The days are shorter, it is true, but remember that each season has beauty. A few hours in the garden with the sharp wind blowing will tinge my cheeks with a ruddy glow and cause the fallen leaves to dance up and down from the ground. I am looking forward to the return of warm sweaters, boots and scarves.

Leaves, leaves, leaves! Try to keep on top of them and collect weekly (see page 219) – you will be finished by next season, I promise!

Even though the outside growing season is over, those true enthusiasts who really want to have something going on may want to sow a few parsley, coriander or basil seeds in pots on a warm light windowsill. There's nothing quite as cheery as a

few edible fresh leaves to garnish a casserole, plate of curry or bowl of pasta.

Split Rhubarb

The rhubarb patch will be looking quite messy as leaves and stalks have died back, turned brown and yellow. It really is a shadow of its former self. If your rhubarb didn't do terribly well it may benefit from being split and now is the time to do it. Similarly, you may have just one rhubarb crown and would like to increase your stocks.

The crown is now asleep for the winter and can be safely dug up and examined. Remove any parts that appear obviously decayed or rotten. The remaining firm and solid crown can be divided by either pulling apart if it is not too large, or using a spade or knife to cut it into clumps about 23cm (9 inches) in size. These pieces can now be replanted and spaced well apart – I allow around 90cm (3 feet) between crowns. Plant them so that the surface of the crown is just at the soil level, then add a top dressing of homemade compost or leaf mould and forget about it. I see small new shoots by the time the winter comes to an end.

Water Spring Flowering Bulbs for Indoor Use

If you potted up spring bulbs for Christmas gifts or for indoor use, start to give them a drink of water so that they will be just right for gifting next month. I like to give them as gifts, not in full flower, but with shoots about 2.5cm (1 inch) tall – something to look forward to when all of the Christmas and holiday decorations have been taken down!

The Luffa Gourd Challenge

Following a long stay of two to three weeks in the airing cupboard, my Luffas dried firm and hard. A shake confirms this as the seeds can be heard rattling around inside. The thick skin breaks off in large shards, rather than peeling away, to reveal the dried fibrous gorgeous shape that I have spent so many years and failed attempts to achieve. Shaking out the seeds took time – they fly around all over the place. I managed to save a good bag full that will be saved over winter then I can try to grow them again next spring. I cut the natural Luffa sponges into 13cm (5 inch) lengths – a handy size for me. Each fruit yielded three Luffa sponges.

Unlike the shop bought pieces, mine are discoloured and will need a thorough clean and whiten before I can put them to good use. This can soon sorted using a quick dip in a green bleach (sodium percarbonate) solution.

TO WHITEN AND STERILISE
1–2 tsp green bleach (sodium percarbonate)
1 litre (34fl oz) of boiling water
large mixing bowl
de-seeded Luffa

Pour the boiling water over the bleach and stir with a wooden spoon until dissolved and activated then add the luffa sponges and leave for 15-20 minutes.

The sponges will bleach to a clean creamy white. Rinse with cold water, press down to make a square shape rather than cylindrical and the Luffas are ready to use.

I am amazed at how robust these little scourers are. They last months, can be bleached again to clean and sterilise from time to time, get wet and dry, wet and dry and never complain. When they do finally give up they can be tossed onto the compost heap, unlike the green plastic sponge alternatives which are not nearly as much fun.

Harvest Raspberries – Autumn Bliss Variety

The Autumn Bliss berries will finish fruiting around this time, though I have been known to harvest a few fresh raspberries on Christmas Eve – it really depends on the weather conditions. The leaves on the tall stems will be yellowing and the fruits well past their prime, so now is the time to cut down the canes. Unlike summer-fruiting varieties, the Autumn Bliss variety are not so fussy. The whole lot is cut down to ground level, leaving stubbles of just 5–7.5cm (2–3 inches) above ground and that's it. Raspberries are a woodland plant, so I then top off the cut-down stubbles with a good top dressing of leaf mould to mimic an autumn fall and leave them for the winter. An additional benefit for the novice gardener is they need no frame or wire supports.

Get Winter Ready

The veggie plot may look like a shadow of its former self. What was several seasons ago a thriving growing space may now be looking barren aside from the brave leeks, kale, sprouts and parsnips who will happily take on whatever winter will throw at them. Those areas of the plot that have served me well I make sure have been cleared of weeds, then my winter preparation takes place. No longer is there the back-breaking job of autumn double digging – the 'green' gardener simply lays a layer of compost on the top.

I know my compost is ready to use when it's a dark, rich colour, crumbles easily and it is impossible to recognise any of the ingredients that went into it. It smells rich and earthy and now comes into its own. (See Create Compost on page 25.)

To 'add back' nutrients that were taken by my crops as they were growing earlier in the year, I spread a 2.5–5cm (1–2 inch) layer of this gorgeous natural loam on the beds, and that's it. What follows then will improve the soil's structure and nutrients. Over the coming weeks and months, the compost-improved soil will retain moisture and air and, thanks to the worms and other organisms who miraculously weave in and out throughout the winter, will make my beds great growing spaces ready for next spring.

DRIED PEAS AND BEANS FOR KITCHEN USE

Any peas and beans you stored when clearing the season's crops should now by dry and ready for shelling. Either pop them into paper bags and store with your supply of seeds for next year or, if you have loads, you can use them from dried in the kitchen too.

One year I found myself with far more runner bean seeds than I needed so popped them into a jar to use through the winter in stews and casseroles. They can be used just like any other dried bean but the satisfaction for me was knowing my beans were organic and even better they were free!

As with any dried bean or pea, it is important to soak them overnight in a bowl of cold water, which helps remove the enzyme that our body cannot fully break down. The soaking helps to get rid of these complex sugars making them easier to digest, therefore reducing gas and indigestion. Soaking also softens the beans and therefore reduces the cooking time. Most beans need to cook for a minimum of 20 minutes until soft and tender. Home dried beans I have found, because they are younger, take less time to cook than their older supermarket counterparts.

Needless to say – absolutely delighted by this free food opportunity that year – I now allow any bean plant (runner beans, French beans, cannellini, borlotti or peas) to grow over-sized pods that then dry on the plant before I then collect all of the seeds.

YOU WILL NEED

dried overgrown bean or pea pods

screw-topped glass jars

wide wicker basket or tray

hairdryer (and an extension lead)

Simply shell the beans and reserve as many as you need for next year's planting.

Sort through remaining beans and remove any damaged, discoloured or non-uniform beans.

The next step is called 'winnowing' which involves the removal of any residual dust and piece of shell. This is quite a fun thing to do and is best done outside. Simply have all of the beans in a wide basket or tray and blow the hairdryer over them. Instantly all of the light loose debris will fly off, leaving just a gorgeous supply of beans

Pop them into the glass jar and secure with a lid. Place the full jar of beans into the freezer for 3 days then leave to return to room temperature, unopened, and store in a cool dry place. I have read that the three-day freezer blast will destroy any microscopic organisms that may have been present on the beans and that could go on to destroy the beans when in store.

THE MINI BONFIRE

While the compost bin is the healthy and wonderful natural dumping ground for most garden waste, there are certain items that need to be burnt in order to eliminate the spreading of disease. I think the occasional garden bonfire to deal with such issues is not a huge environmental hazard, though always check with your local authority to ensure there are no strict rules about fires to be observed.

A garden bonfire shouldn't be a huge roaring, out of hand, black smoking affair that annoys the neighbours on a sunny warm Sunday afternoon. Many years ago, I had a neighbour who religiously lit a bonfire at the weekend and burnt just paper on it – it used to drive me mad!

A garden bonfire, I think, needs to be a rare occurrence and should only be lit for a specific purpose – like my poor, diseased blackcurrant bushes mentioned on page 20. I needed to eliminate this problem quickly and effectively.

There are custom-made incinerator bins that look a bit like an old-fashioned galvanised dustbin on legs but then – looking close up – it has holes in the side and a chimney in the lid. These are perfect for a small, quick effective, non-dangerous, well-controlled bonfire. An old metal dustbin or metal container lifted onto bricks will also work well, though be sure it hadn't been used to store something flammable and always take all necessary precautions.

‖‖

TIP: The resultant wood ash from a garden fire can be a useful dry layer to the compost heap or can be applied directly to the ground. It can be a natural source of potassium and trace elements and a sprinkle around the bases of apples, currants and gooseberries in the spring will be much appreciated when the rain washes it down to their roots.

‖‖

HOME-MADE FIRELIGHTERS

Lighting a bonfire produces less smoke if heat is generated quickly – I make these simple little firelighters with reused household items.

Makes 6 firelighters

YOU WILL NEED
scrap paper or newspaper
burnt down or spent candles (you will need enough for 5–6
    tbsp grated wax)
potato peeler
small baked bean tin or other aluminium can
small saucepan
kettle of boiling water
used egg box
chopping board
airtight bag or tin

Lay a piece of paper on a work surface and work at a spent candle with a potato peeler to remove small shards or gratings from the spent candles. Take the used, washed and dried aluminium can and give it a squeeze so that the can takes on an oval shape – this will provide a perfect 'pourer' for the melted wax.

Scoop up the piece of wax-filled paper to form a funnel and transfer to the oval-shaped tin. Stand the tin in a small saucepan, pour boiling water around the side and leave to stand for several minutes until the wax melts. If it fails to melt completely, place the pan over a low heat on the hob until the wax melts and is clear and runny.

During the minutes when the wax is melting, tightly scrunch up some small pieces of scrap paper or newspaper (not shiny magazine paper as it doesn't ignite well) and force it into the cups of the egg box as tightly as you can. Then take the tin of melted wax from the pan of water and – using the oval-shaped tin – pour the wax from cup to cup in the egg box. Leave the wax to set completely then place the very hard egg box onto a chopping board and cut (I used a knife) into six pieces. Wrap each piece in a parcel using another square of scrap paper or newspaper, store in an airtight bag or tin to keep dry. When you need to light your bonfire, a quick light of the touch-paper is all that is required. Keep the wax tin for next time – don't ever be tempted to use a favourite jug or pan to melt wax – you'll never get it out!

WINTER

EARLY WINTER

I f there has not yet been an overnight frost, there's every chance one will come early this season. Fewer daylight hours results in life being very much lived indoors, with lots of Christmas, holiday and seasonal preparation and maybe not much thought given to the garden.

Although the days are short there are still opportunities when a few jobs can be tackled. The most I will probably do, on a dry and clear day, is gather up a few evergreen pieces such as holly branches and sprigs, lengths of bay, spruce, rose-hips, pine cones, dried hydrangea heads and grasses. Tied together and displayed in a vase, they make a long-lasting seasonal display so there's no need to brighten the house with a shop- or supermarket-bought bouquet of unseasonal, imported flowers.

If you haven't already, cover your garden furniture – I often stack mine in the greenhouse and try to make the garden, its buildings, plants and trees as weatherproof as I can.

And some planning, planting and harvesting can still take place, too. As much as I thoroughly enjoy the bumper harvests of the plentiful seasons of summer and autumn, winter harvesting is very precious. I have, of course, my jars of pickles, my stored onions, beetroot and potatoes, and my freezers have sufficient produce to see me through, but there is still the thrill of harvesting outside.

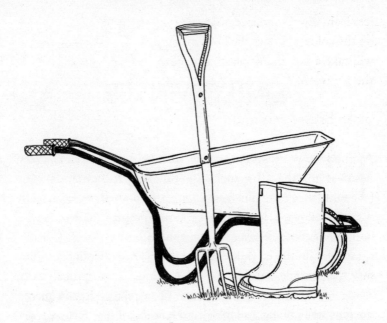

I carefully choose the veggies that I grow for harvesting during the winter – old faithfuls that I know can put their backs to the wind, sit there for many weeks and take whatever the weather throws at them. The advantage of these crops is that I can harvest just what I need – I may only need one leek or parsnip to add to a stew, maybe only half a dozen sprouts if I am home alone – and kale is king when it comes to fresh winter greens.

Seasonal Tip for Birds

Time, also, to not forget about the birds, and if you like to attract wild birds into your garden then the feeders probably need to be refilled two or three times a week. Remember too that bird baths and troughs need to be kept clean and free of

ice. I am always amazed that even
on the coldest of days the bold robin
will take a dip and a splash around in
the icy water.

Stake Brussels Sprouts

A good crop of sprouts may well be
destined for the Christmas dinner plate
(some say they taste much sweeter after their first frost). Make
sure the tall plants are well staked and, once the 'buttons' have
been harvested, remember to eat the leafy tops too. One leafy
sprout top is just the right amount of free fresh greens to serve
four – boiled, steamed or stir-fried.

Once a sprout stem has been fully stripped, pull it out of
the ground and – instead of tossing it straight into the compost
– use a spade to chop it into 15cm (6 inch) lengths. It will
then decompose evenly and much quicker.

Harvest Kale

Kale is a fantastic crop for the winter months. The plants are
small and compact, and a row or two – resembling a forest of
mini trees with their dark green crinkly leaves – will keep the
kitchen supplied for months. Highly nutritious and versatile,
it can be served simply boiled or steamed as a winter green
vegetable, cooked and stirred into pasta, or blanched and incor-
porated into a home-made pesto.

When harvesting, take a few leaves from each plant, starting
at the bottom and working upwards: that way you will harvest
for longer. At the same time, if you see any yellowing, dropped

and decayed leaves, remove those too to ensure good air circulation around the plant. Pop any debris lying around onto the compost heap.

Harvest Leeks

When it comes to harvesting leeks I favour a small garden fork and use it to lightly unhinge the roots from the soil. Don't be tempted to simply pull at the leek. Even though it may not look deep rooted, those little roots are firmly fixed and pulling at the top will cause the leek to snap, leaving the roots and white in the ground and you will be left holding the green! Once out of the ground, shake off any excess soil then you can cut off the larger roots and pop them into the compost bin. The green tops should be trimmed and the outside leaves peeled off revealing perfect white and green gorgeousness.

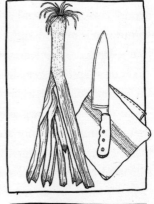

A quick dig for a leek on the worst winter day can be a swift affair. On with my wellies and waterproofs, and with a small garden fork I can easily uplift a leek then run back inside to prepare it. Cut off the roots and the top 7.5–10cm (3–4 inches) of the green leaves. I like to eat the whole of the veg, not just

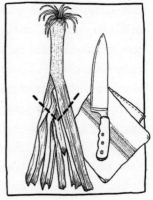

the white part. After removing one or two of the bedraggled outside leaves – this is how I clean it.

Take a vegetable knife in one hand with the point facing away from you. Hold the leek with the white part uppermost and the green leaves below in the other hand. Pierce the leek at the place where the white becomes green then, in one continuous movement upwards, pull the knife from top to bottom thereby splicing the green part of the leek. The leaves can now be fanned open and washed well, removing every trace of dirt while keeping the leek in one piece. Shake to remove excess moisture then slice and use as required.

Sometimes, if I am showing off or want to gift a few, I like to perfect the appearance of my harvested leeks and I can best describe the finished specimen looking like a green pointed arrow. After removing the roots and peeling off the outside scruffy looking leaves I then trim the mass of green to a point using a knife. Work from the outside leaves to the centre from both sides finishing with a centre point. Your leek will look so smart, tidy and beautiful, setting it apart from its shop bought supermarket neighbours.

Even though my home-grown leek will now look resplendent it still needs to be washed well. Among all of those tightly wrapped leaves there will be grit and dirt – I have even had sycamore seeds tucked down there!

Harvest Parsnips

There are times I may need just one parsnip, and others I may need a basketful, yet going outside to uproot one or more fresh from the garden is priceless. They may not be picture perfect specimens, and there is always mystery and intrigue plus a twinge of excitement when harvesting them: will this one be a whopper, have two legs or be short and stubby? On the surface they look the same and it's not until I carefully dig deep down to loosen the precious root that the truth will be revealed. There is nothing quite like the thrill of digging up a perfectly shaped parsnip, full and robust at the top then tapering off gradually to a point – like a huge ice-cream cone. Once cleaned and washed, I always take a second or two to admire its long journey (in more ways than one!) – this girl has been living below ground for almost a year!

I am not, by the way, ignoring the not-so-perfect little fat stubby ones or those with two legs because they will taste just as good too!

When harvesting a parsnip, I use a spade rather than a fork and place the spade a good six to eight inches away from where the root is. So many times over the years I have forced a fork prong into the root or, at worst, cut through it altogether. By placing the spade away from the root, you are lifting the soil which at the same time loosens the root, then it is possible to lift the whole veg without causing damage.

Plant Garlic, Onions and Shallots – it's not too late!

On a mild day, provided the ground is not too wet or hard with frost, garlic, onion and shallot bulbs can be still be planted. The best time is from late autumn to early winter (garlic can be planted up to midwinter) and, just like spring flowering bulbs, garlic, onion and shallots planted before the winter quickly develop roots and the little plants are well established before the very cold weather which will slow down their growing. See page 220 for more details.

Plan Your Raspberries

If you are planning a row of summer-fruiting raspberries, you'll require a frame for training them once they start growing. This is a great cooler weather job, for a fine and dry day when you want to get outside and do something other than picking up fallen leaves! Start instead on your plan for next year.

A wooden post at each end of the row and three wires spaced evenly at 91cm, 1.2m, 1.5m (3 foot, 4 foot and 5 foot) will provide space for the growing canes to be tied on and protected from winds and prevent clusters of berries falling to the ground. Imagine your frame for the summer canes looking similar to a pair of 2-metre (6-foot) high telegraph poles with three evenly spaced wires starting halfway up. A raspberry cane needs quite a lot of space, so allow 46–60cm (18–24 inches) per plant – you'll not need many per row.

REDUCE, REUSE AND RECYCLE

Keep an eye out for handy containers that can be used as planters in the spring. Christmas and holiday times are ideal, as packaging is in abundance! I always keep back those sturdy shallow cardboard trays often used to pack small oranges. They make the perfect tray for holding cardboard tubes, which I am also busy scurrying to find and set aside. Here are ideas for other forms of packaging that can be given a new lease of life in the garden.

TIP: Remember plain cardboard, paper and packaging can be added to the compost pile rather than added to general refuse. See Create Compost on page 25.

Loo-roll superstar

Upcycled cardboard tubes make the perfect growing pot for plants that grow a long tap root, such as sweet peas and garden peas. Offering a tall, narrow vessel for the seed to grow in is perfect for so many reasons. Firstly, it is free, secondly the plant can grow without constraint, and thirdly, the whole lot can be planted out when required – there's no turning out of the pot, no root disturbance and the cardboard will simply decompose, never to be seen again.

Every year I plant seeds for sweet peas and garden peas in tubes and they stand upright perfectly in the sturdy cardboard trays (See the sweet pea seasonal special on page 287.) Experiment with other seeds too, especially large seeds such as nasturtiums, beans and courgettes.

Thinking outside the 'plastic' box

Keep those single-use clear plastic containers baby tomatoes, blueberries and other small fruits are sold in – they make perfect planting pots or trays. Many already have ventilation holes in the base, which will double-up as drainage holes when used for sowing seeds. I have even had success in crafting and creating a mini propagator which helped to germinate tomato seeds – it was simply a clear plastic tray with holes in, plus a lid which fitted on top exactly. Originally it was a closed container of green seedless grapes.

There are many possibilities for the first-time grower that will not cost the earth. When it comes to plant labels, there are a number of everyday items that can be upcycled. Wooden lolly sticks make fantastic labels and a washed-out cream or yoghurt pot can be cut in half, the bottom cut out then divided into strips to use as plant labels rather than having to go out and buy custom-made ones. I manage to make twelve good-sized plant labels from one 300ml (10fl oz) carton.

FRUIT TREE WINTER WASH

If you have fruit trees, you may have read about a 'winter wash', which helps control the overwintering of insects, bugs and aphid eggs. I have two cherry trees in the garden, and one has produced lots of gorgeous cherries every summer for several years. I decided to add to my stocks (who doesn't love cherries!) and invested in a small ornamental patio black Morello cherry tree – the fruits are dark red, large and although they are described as being more acidic than other cherries, mine are sweet and gorgeous. Patio trees are a great idea for those with a small space. I bought the tree in the winter and when the spring arrived the buds burst, the blossom arrived, but so did the black cherry aphid. Seemingly overnight, the new bright green leaves were covered in a sticky substance which had caused them to curl up, turn brown and begin to wither and die. When I examined them closely, I realised this substance was a huge infestation of shiny tiny black beetle-like aphids. I have a natural remedy for treating these little blighters along with other aphids and greenfly in my book *Clean & Green*, but having had this problem the previous summer – now is the time to prevent the same happening again.

About every two to three weeks or at least once a month, from now and until the growing season arrives in spring, I will spray my little tree with my home-mixed 'winter wash', which helps to prevent the overwintering eggs from hatching out in the springtime.

Now is the time to inspect your other fruit trees too, particularly the soft stone-fruit trees such as plum, apricot, greengage and damson. If you see any weeping areas or patches that seem to be growing fungus, give them a spray too. My apricot tree is probably twenty years old, and for the first few years gave me quite a good crop of apricots, but then the fruiting stopped. Year after year I got lots of leaf and beautiful blossom but no fruits. Last year, however, I had an abundance of apricots and I'm not sure why. It could have been the weather conditions, it may have been my winter wash which had dried up an area of canker (a bacterial disease which shows as a shiny, sticky substance on branches of fruit trees) or it may just have been a good year for apricots.

When the spring arrives and the buds begin to fatten, I will cease the spraying and my tree should be free to flourish, blossom, welcome the bees and other pollinators and then fruit without the inconvenience of the little monsters.

TIP: Neem Oil is a natural insect repellent and is used in many organic pesticides but has an unpleasant smell, a short shelf life, and can be expensive so I have found this cocktail works just as well.

Mindful that winter spraying can be harmful to overwintering beneficial insects such as ladybirds, I restrict my spraying to only those trees where I have had problems, for instance a plum tree that had managed to house a maggot in every fruit. All other trees, bushes and shrubs I leave untouched, aware that they may be long-stay hotels for my garden's insects.

YOU WILL NEED
200ml tepid water
3 drops eco-friendly washing-up liquid
2 drops rosemary essential oil
2 drops clove-bud oil
small spray bottle

Put all the ingredients in the bottle then give it a shake. The eco-friendly washing-up liquid helps to emulsify the oil with the water so that the mix clings to the trunk and branches of the tree.

This recipe is for a small mix – enough for two to three small trees – though if you have lots of fruit trees, double or triple the quantities as required. I make up a fresh bottle each time. Examine your fruit trees and look for signs of fungus or mossy areas and spray onto any cracks in the bark and other areas, particularly on ornamental trees where grafting has taken place (grafting is a form of propagating new fruit trees using buds or twigs; it is, in its simplest of terms, joining two plants into one) – you will see the 'join' on the main trunk. I am sure this is where my overwintering black cherry aphid eggs had collected – so I made sure to give this area a good spray.

SEASONAL DECORATIONS

A winter walk or just a stroll around the garden will reveal lots of natural seasonal decoration opportunities. Pine cones, sprigs of holly and ivy, hawthorn berries, rosehips, a few loose sprigs from a Christmas tree – all will add natural colour and texture to even the simplest of Christmas items.

For a few years I have resisted bright, shiny, glittery Christmas wrapping paper and have reused brown parcel wrapping paper instead. I iron flat any pieces that are heavily creased then use Christmas-themed rubber stamps to decorate the paper. It looks unbelievably beautiful, secured with biodegradable brown sticky tape, wrapped in jute twine (biodegradable string), a gift tag upcycled from last year's Christmas cards and finished with a sprig of holly – what's not to like? When the frantic session of gift-opening is finished – rather than the wrappings being gathered up and thrown into the bin to end their days in landfill – mine are gathered up and I then salvage longer lengths of string, large sheets of paper that can be used again then the rest is added as a 'dry layer' to my compost bin.

Christmas Tree

As there is lots going on in the run-up to Christmas, let us give a thought to the Christmas tree. There are many good artificial trees on the market, but I have to admit I adore the scent and 'realness' of a natural Christmas tree. A living Christmas tree is beautiful and nostalgic but nowadays can be incredibly expensive. I have seen them available to buy in stores as early as late autumn: the poor things... goodness knows when they were felled, they have no root, they've been suffocated and squashed into tight plastic netting and the ones that don't appeal will presumably be left to wither and die.

I have a number of Christmas trees in the garden and all have been grown from babies. Each year one of them comes into the house to be decorated and is then returned to its home in the ground after just over two weeks.

I dig it up with a good ball of soil attached, creating as little disturbance as possible, and pop it into a large, free-draining pot – any large-enough container is perfect as long as it has holes in the base for excess water to escape. The tree will be given a full litre (34fl oz) of water every day, so the pot needs to stand on a tray to catch any excess so that any carpet or wooden flooring or table isn't left stained.

The atmosphere is dry, and the house is very warm compared to outside, so I place the tree in the cool hallway and away from radiators. When deciding on a tree to bring inside, try to remember that it looks smaller in the ground than it will look when it has been dug up, lifted into a pot and taken indoors and decorated, so err on the side of caution when it comes to size. I once helped to bring in a huge tree that took out two bulbs from the ceiling light fitting as it was being taken to its corner spot in the hall.

The usual timetable for me is that the tree comes in on the 15th December and is returned home on the 1st January. The tree doesn't dry out and I haven't had one die on me yet.

||||||||||||||||||||||||||||||||||||||||||||||||||||||||||||||||||||||||||||||||||||||||||||||||||||||||

TIP: A potted tree can be decorated inside and then
found a place outside once the festivities are over.
Such a tree makes a great gift idea too.

||||||||||||||||||||||||||||||||||||||||||||||||||||||||||||||||||||||||||||||||||||||||||||||||||||||||

A small tree in a pot will soon grow to be a large specimen. If you want to start growing your own for future years, a tiny 30cm (12 inch) tree in a pot will be a spectacle in 3–4 years.

A Christmas tree planted outside in a good deep hole slightly larger than the pot itself and then filled in with compost needs little attention and once it gets used to the extra space will be sprouting lime green tips in no time. For the first year it is necessary to keep the tree well-watered, once a week from planting, even though the weather may be wet, and especially during the summer months when it could easily be forgotten.

TIP: Rather than bringing a tree inside, a Christmas tree
in a prominent place in a larger garden can be
decorated with outdoor lights, then 'passers-by'
can enjoy it too.

LEMON AND PEPPER KALE CRISPS

Try making a batch of these crisps – a super-healthy seasonal nibble – when the oven has been on for something else. Once I have removed my cake, pie or casserole, I then slide in the sheets of kale, resetting the oven to 80-100°C (Gas Mark ¼/ 200°F).

YOU WILL NEED
sharp vegetable knife
colander
clean tea towel
large mixing bowl
grater or microplane
mini whisk or fork
1 or 2 baking trays
reusable baking parchment

100g (3½oz) fresh kale
½ tbsp rapeseed or olive oil
1 tbsp freshly ground black pepper
finely grated zest of 1 lemon
sprinkle of salt

Preheat the oven to 100°C (Gas Mark ¼/210°F), if it's not already on from cooking something else.

Strip the kale leaves off the stalks and cut the leaves with a sharp vegetable knife into roughly 5cm (2 inch) pieces. Wash well in cold salted water – adding salt to the water immediately detaches any over-wintering insects and they'll sink to the bottom of the bowl. Drain the kale in a colander then pat dry on a clean tea towel.

Put the oil, pepper and lemon zest in the mixing bowl and whisk with a mini whisk or fork, then add the kale. Work the lemon and oil into the leaves with your hands until each one is coated and glossy.

Divide between the two baking sheets. Bake in the oven for 1-2 hours, and keep checking to make sure the leaves are still dark green in colour and shiny. When they are super crispy, they are done. Remove from the oven and sprinkle with salt – they are delicious and will stay crispy for days.

PARSNIP CHOCOLATE CHIP LOAF

During the winter months, parsnips are plentiful in the garden and in the shops. If you struggle to persuade children to eat them, try this cake. My grandson, when eating a slice one time, was asked whether he liked it: 'I love this cake, Granny – my favourite is always chocolate and banana!' This cake is truly lovely – moist, tasty and light. Parsnips are naturally sweet and therefore there's no need to add much refined sugar. It is easy to make and will keep well for at least a week in an airtight tin.

Makes 1 loaf

YOU WILL NEED
food processor fitted with grater attachment, or regular
    grater
large mixing bowl
whisk
900g (2lb) loaf tin, greased and lined

180g (6oz) trimmed parsnip (core and skin removed)
150ml (5fl oz) flavourless oil (I use vegetable or sunflower)
125g (4¼oz) caster sugar
3 eggs
1 tsp vanilla extract
180g (6oz) self-raising flour
½ tsp ground nutmeg
100g (3½oz) dark chocolate chips
icing sugar, for dusting

Preheat the oven to 190°C (Gas Mark 5/375°F).

Grate the trimmed parsnips very finely (I use a machine) then set aside. The more finely grated it is, the more the parsnip becomes part of the cake crumb and avoids being detected by picky eaters!

Put the oil, sugar and eggs in a large mixing bowl and whisk for about 3 minutes until well combined. Add the vanilla extract then sift over the flour and nutmeg. Fold in the flour until almost combined, then add the grated parsnip and chocolate chips. Stir well until everything comes together then transfer to the prepared loaf tin.

Bake for 1 hour–1 hour 10 minutes until the cake is risen, golden brown and firm to the touch.

Remove from the oven, leave to cool in the tin for 20 minutes, then turn out onto a wire rack to cool completely. A dusting of icing sugar is all it needs to look fabulous!

If you want to batch bake this cake then it will freeze well.

||||||||||||||||||||||||||||||||||||||||||||||||||||||||||||||||||||||||||||||||||||||||||||||||||||||||||||||||||||||||

TIP: I routinely turn the oven off at least 10 minutes before the end of any prescribed cooking time. Provided the oven door remains closed, there is sufficient residual heat to complete the job. This even works for those foods which require the hottest of ovens, i.e., bread and Yorkshire puddings!

||||||||||||||||||||||||||||||||||||||||||||||||||||||||||||||||||||||||||||||||||||||||||||||||||||||||||||||||||||||||

MIDWINTER

B y now, the festive season is over, and the days are short and often cold and dark. We may have snow, or are just as likely to have an un-seasonal mild spell, but whatever the weather, midwinter can often seem a little endless. There will be a few clearing-up jobs to do in the garden, but by and large most of the time the weather determines that you stay indoors and, when that is the case, I like to cheer myself up by thinking about the year to come and start to think about the garden and plan my planting.

Winter is the perfect opportunity to make notes about the veggies, fruits and flowers you would like to grow. As an aide memoire, I peruse last year's A4 garden diary and remind myself of notes I made about changes I had planned, crops that had done well, etc. It may be that you had such a good year last year with one crop that you want more and need to extend the growing area.

With this in mind, it is fun on a crisp, dry day to get outside and do a bit of planning. Maybe, if you have thought about trying more and different crops now that you have the growing bug, it is a good time to measure your plan or plot. At this time of year, when the ground looks barren and bare, measuring is easy. Try measuring up various options. Transfer your thoughts to paper and then, when warm and cosy indoors, you can firm up your thoughts and ideas into a plan – a plan to be changed I am sure, but you can make a good start.

Alternatively, for the small space gardener, look at the number of pots and containers that you have and whether you can fit more onto your sunny balcony, patio or other outside space. Remember to use walls and shelving – not everything has to stand on the ground.

It is surprising how quickly time flies by when you get busy, get moving and get warm, even on the coldest of days. I love

spending a cold winter's day outside and then, in the evening, feeling a rosy glow following a hot meal. It's much better for my wellbeing than a day spent indoors, with no fresh air, feeling cramped up, sludgy and dull. Whatever the weather, I get outside for at least an hour a day, even if it is simply for a brisk walk with the dog (even in the pouring rain).

Pine and citrus freebie!

Before discarding a real but cut rather than potted Christmas tree, clip off a few end branches and pop them into a jar of white vinegar with a few strips of orange peel. Leave a few days or up to a week and you have a pungent pine and citrus-fragranced cleaning vinegar. This fabulous concentrated eco-friendly cleaner, made with the scented vinegar, is great for washing pots, trays, outdoor furniture – in fact anything! I use it inside the house too, diluted with hot water, to clean my floors.

YOU WILL NEED

200ml (7fl oz) pine- and citrus-infused vinegar

50ml (1¾fl oz) eco-friendly washing-up liquid

20–30 drops organic rosemary or orange oil, for a stronger
    perfume (optional)

300ml (10fl oz) bottle

Simply add all the ingredients to the bottle,
seal and shake. Add 2 tablespoons to a bucket
before adding hot tap water to dilute.

Harvest

My Brussels sprout harvest may be almost done for the year.
However, my kale is still going strong, as are leeks and parsnips.
By this time, parsnip tops have died down to nothing, but the
strong healthy roots are still sitting patiently in the soil,
remaining fresh and good to eat. I adore growing leeks and
parsnips because I can harvest as few or as many at a time as
I need, and one of the best advantages is that I am still
harvesting last year's crop as I begin to think about sowing
this year's.

The Sunny Side

As part of your planning, think about the sun and shade and
plan your crops accordingly. What may seem an open sunny
position in the winter may change by the time that tree next
door is in full leaf. Have a look around – the sunny spot you
first thought of may not be the best place.

Similarly, if you would like to grow climbing beans or sweet-corn, for example, or anything that can grow as high as 1.8–2.5m (6–8ft), make sure it doesn't then create a huge wall of shade over a row of tomatoes that you planted next door that really need that full sun. I try, where I can, to grow tall crops such as these at the northern end of the plot so that they cast their shadow onto a non-veg growing area. Have a think about when and where the sun arrives into your garden and any buildings, sheds or trees that may affect and interrupt the sunshine. There are 'sun calculator' websites available that, wherever you are in the world, let you check out where and when the sun and shade will be in your own garden in any given season. They don't take into account natural obstructions, but they are a very good place to start!

A veggie plot needs as much full sun as possible, so positioning your plot in a north-facing aspect and/or among shade from large trees or buildings should be avoided. See my section on Companion Planting too (page 114) to further understand how crops grown together can deter certain insects and pests, can share rather than compete for the soil's available nutrients, and how some can actually help each other to flourish.

PICKING YOUR SEEDS FOR THE YEAR

For those fairly new to gardening, just starting out or who are impatient and want to buy a few packets of seeds to cherish in readiness for warmer weather, I recommend the following. Each are easy to grow, don't take up much space and will give you more joy than you ever expected – when ready to harvest, you can just take what you need. These are all good in pots or boxes and will each get off to a trouble-free start.

FOREVER FRIENDS
courgette
radish
spring onion
salad leaves
carrot
basil
parsley
rocket
tomatoes

Decide on your choice of seeds or small plants and either order them online or take a trip to your favourite garden centre to have a browse. Each year I look through my own stock of bought and saved seed to check whether they are still in date and that they are free flowing, dry and not subject to any mould. When the time arrives, rather than sowing 'out of date' seeds into the ground or maybe seeds that have been given to you and you're unsure of their history, start them off in a tray or pots and in that way you will not be wasting valuable space if they fail to germinate. I cannot tell you how many times I have secured a valuable section of the garden, planted a row of old seeds, left them for weeks and then nothing has emerged. That piece of land could have been growing well by now had I used new or fresh seeds or started them off in a tray or pots.

Old parsnip seeds are unlikely to germinate, but many others will do very well when well past their 'use by' date. I had a packet of pea seeds that were two years out of date and, rather than sowing them directly into the ground, I popped them into cardboard tubes (you could also use small pots). Every single one germinated – fantastic! The tubes were then planted into neat rows, with not a gap in sight. I have decided this is my way forward with peas as I rarely achieve 100 per cent germination when I sow direct into the ground.

After buying your choice of seeds, take a look at the back of the packets and check that there is plenty of time before sowing needs to begin. The earliest most packets will tell you to get started is probably late winter/early spring, and there is usually a three-month planting window, so no rush!

There are many varieties to choose from, so if I can't see my favourite varieties it's an opportunity to try something different. These varieties have germinated well for me and produced good crops. Packets of seeds can be pricey, so I am increasingly saving seed from my own harvest (see parsnip and runner bean seeds pages 47 and 215), sharing with friends and choosing varieties with a good 'use by' date.

In addition to the previous list, for those unsure which varieties to choose, these are a few 'failsafe', easy, high yielding options.

Salad leaves – try the 'cut and come again' selections which will keep going for several weeks

Radish – French breakfast

Spring onion – white Lisbon

Courgette – will grow in the ground or in a pot and a single plant can produce up to 50 fruits – the bright yellow flowers are edible too. Try a packet of seeds with a mix of colours, e.g. BBQ Mixed

Tomato – Gardener's Delight will grow outside or under glass, will produce tasty tomatoes and will grow in any soil. Marmande are huge beefy tomatoes that are a meal in themselves in a good year, great fresh and for sauces. Flavour wise, they're my favourite.

Potatoes – Second Early and Charlotte are now my favourite varieties because they store well too

Broad beans – Bunyard's Exhibition because they can be
   sown in autumn or spring
French Beans – Compass
Runner beans – Scarlet Emperor. I have used my own seed
   since buying a packet of seeds many years ago. High
   yielding, bright scarlet edible flowers and they will
   produce more beans than you can manage!
For the cut-flower lover – sweet peas and cosmos

Don't be afraid to try something new if there is a crop you
really fancy – decide on your favourite veggies and just go for
it! Remember, even though the results may not be show-
condition they will be edible however small or misshapen.
Don't be put off.

You can purchase your packets of seeds any time from now
until sowing time, which can be up to late spring. However,

for one crop – the potato – midwinter is the time to buy. Seed potatoes need some six weeks or so to prepare before they are ready to plant into the ground in early spring.

CHITTING POTATOES

I buy First Earlies, which as their name suggests are the first of the new season's crop. Choose any variety that takes your fancy, but I highly recommend Charlotte. I always used to grow *Arran Pilot* simply because my grandad did, but Charlotte now has my vote. They're easy to grow in pots, too. I harvest them small to eat with salads then leave a row in the ground to harvest in midsummer and, after curing (see page 145), they keep me in large potatoes well into the autumn. Potatoes are very easy to grow – even planting a sprouted potato from your veg drawer will produce a crop.

Growing potatoes has become a passion for me, and even though I have grown them for many years, I continue to learn and understand more about them. I devoted a whole chapter to the gorgeous spud in *Green Living Made Easy* and a plan for the future is to grow maincrop potatoes that I can store for winter use.

Once you get your bag of seed potatoes home, look for a large egg box or shallow cardboard tray and choose a cool, light, frost-free place for your potatoes. I set mine out in a box on a wide window ledge in a north-facing pantry. It is cool, very light and frost free. For the next six weeks they will be left to 'chit' (sprout). This fun activity simply involves taking your small potatoes from their packaging and setting them out on the egg box (because it holds them upright) so that they can begin 'chitting' before they are planted into the ground in early spring.

If they are left in their packet they will still sprout, but instead of strong sturdy growth you would get long, white shoots which would wrap themselves all around the potatoes as they struggle, searching for light. Have you ever had a bag of eating potatoes from the shop which have been forgotten about and, when you inspect them some time later, they have started to sprout white roots and shoots? The same thing will happen to the seed potatoes if not given space and light.

At first, the seed potato will simply look like a small, ordinary, rather wrinkled potato but if you get up close you will notice that at one end there is a tiny dry string which is where it was once attached to the mother plant (this is the bottom of the potato), and around the rest of the potato are tiny 'eyes', mini dimples in the skin. It is from these eyes that shoots will start to grow upwards.

Stand the potato with its bottom in the egg box so that the shoots when they start to grow will be heading upwards in the right direction. If you happen to put your potato in the box upside down, you will notice that the shoots will try to do a U-turn in order to grow upwards. Once you spot this you can flip them the right way up. Your 'chitting' potatoes will take six to eight weeks to be ready for planting. The dark green compact sprouts will be about half an inch tall when ready to be planted in early spring.

THE GREAT GARDEN CLEAN-UP

A mild spell in mid to late winter is the ideal opportunity to have a clean-up. Even though the ground may be too hard or too wet to work, having a browse around the garden at this time of the year does make me realise that a garden needs time to sleep and recover following the hard work that went into producing food the previous year. Having said that, as the garden now is pretty much a blank canvas now is a great time to consider anything you want to change, expand or just move around. While you have a good browse, pick up dead sticks and fallen bits as you go and inspect them: are they sturdy and long enough to use as pea sticks later on? If so, collect them up, wrap them in a bale with string then you will be good to go when your climbers are ready to be planted in spring.

You may spot a blown-over and cracked or broken pot. Rescue the plant inside and gather up the shards of clay or earthenware. They can be broken up into smaller pieces and stored in a large container in the shed to use as crocks in large pots when transplanting containers.

You may spot a section of fence or trellis that needs a simple repair. Make a note on your 'jobs to do' list or, if it isn't a huge task, get on and do it now as there will be so much to do once the garden wakes up.

The biggest job for me at this time is the inside of the shed and the greenhouse. I may have cleared my greenhouse of plants the previous autumn and arranged my shed into some sort of semblance of order but then somehow it so often becomes a dumping ground or workshop after then. Any

Christmas crafting tends to be done in the greenhouse or shed, and I may have left a trail of cut-off bits and string. There may also be discarded plant pots, seed trays, labels and the like.

Just as a good kitchen cupboard or pantry clear-out and tidy-up improves our performance once everything has been given a place, creating some order, the same is absolutely true for the garden.

In the shed, for example, even if – for the time being – you only have a limited supply of tools, rather than simply standing them upright in a corner you could add a number of hanging hooks. You can buy purpose-made ones, but even several pairs of 7.5–10cm (3–4in) screws secured around the top batten of the shed will do an amazing job, then the 'T' handles of the garden fork, hoe and spade can be suspended and hung from them so that each tool has its own place. Gone will be the days when you reach for the fork from the collection of other tool handles in the corner of the shed only for the whole lot to fall all over the floor. Also, with the tools hung up, there is more floor space available for stacking pots, trays, watering cans, and so on.

For the container gardener, even if you only have a hand trowel and a fork, the little holes in the handles are there so that you can suspend them on screws or hooks in a handy place. If everything has a home you are less likely to misplace them.

When you have been a grower for some time, you will have accumulated lots of pots. Just as kitchen mixing bowls are stored in an orderly manner, with small ones inside larger ones, I do the same with plant pots and containers. Make sure your pots and containers are clean, stack them neatly once dried, and you will be making the best use of available space and it is easy to see what you have on the shelf. A few hours on a cold sunny day splashing about outside with pots and a brush will ensure your crops will be germ- and disease-free later on.

After brushing off any cobwebs, dust and debris, use the brush dipped in the Pure Magic solution to scrub away at your pots and containers. The vinegar in the mix will kill any germs and help to clean everything up. Leave the washed containers once clean out in the sunshine and fresh air. Any residual suds can be rinsed off using a watering can of rainwater.

For badly water-stained or lime-scaled items – pots, planters, bird baths and walk areas that are covered in green algae or mould – Pure Magic will instantly restore your items to their former glory.

A tidy, well organised, shelved and 'tool tidy' shed is a thing of beauty! I enjoy a thorough outdoor session and, once the shed is organised, I like to turn to the greenhouse. I empty the whole thing – a bit like the prep that goes on in the house before setting out to decorate a room. I take out the staging, any pots, bags of compost, trays, watering cans – the whole lot. What I am left with is lots of cobwebs, green algae on the windows, a few weeds growing up through the cracks in the path and even more weeds maybe sneaking up through the gravel. A thorough clean doesn't need to involve high-pressure sprayers, harmful chemical insecticides or disinfectants – this is how I do mine.

First, I clear off debris, cobwebs and overwintering insects with a soft brush and brush the walls and windows, frames and corners, then brush everything onto a shovel and take it outside. What I am left with is a dust- and debris-free empty shell.

The main unsightly issue to be tackled next is the green algae that accumulates on the glazing, some of the wooden areas and in any place that sits in the shade. I don't believe this algae is harmful, though I have read it can steal valuable nutrients from plants; for me more importantly, it significantly reduces the amount of light entering the greenhouse and in its unsightly state makes my greenhouse appear unloved and uncared for. A quick spray of Pure Magic, leave for a few minutes to take hold then wipe and a rinse to quickly tackle any algae. Repeat as necessary for badly affected areas.

An annual clean is the most effective way to eradicate destructive pests, maximise light levels and keep plants healthy. Don't be tempted by plastic-packaged proprietary cleaning products – the simple combination of my old favourite Pure Magic, an old cloth and cold water will do an amazing job. Followers and readers of my other books will be familiar with the wonder of Pure Magic. If anyone ever asks me what my greatest achievement in life has been, the development of the recipe for Pure Magic is up there! This simple spray is a life-changer and I continue to discover more and more uses for it. What started life as an eco-friendly swap for chlorine bleach for toilet cleaning is now used extensively around the home – and garden!

PURE MAGIC GREENHOUSE CLEAN

This gentle giant has developed over each of my books. It is a beast of a cleaning product yet is safe, non-toxic, inexpensive and – most importantly – it does the job. Citric acid kills germs, cuts through algae, mould and moss, and does a great job of cleaning. I add the eco-friendly washing-up liquid as an emulsifier for the oils, which contain antifungal properties too, as well as giving the spray a clean fresh smell.

Sufficient to clean a large greenhouse

YOU WILL NEED
100g (3½oz) citric acid
heatproof measuring jug
75ml (2½fl oz) boiling water
15ml eco-friendly washing-up liquid
4–5 drops organic rosemary, clove-bud or lemon essential oil (optional)
300ml (10fl oz) spray bottle

Measure the citric acid into a heatproof measuring jug (I use Pyrex) then pour over the boiling water and stir until the solution becomes absolutely crystal clear. This is a very important step – if the diluent (diluting agent) is not completely clear, then crystals of citric acid will re-form, multiply and set as a solid lump in the base of the bottle. If this does happen, all is not lost: simply stand the bottle on a warm radiator or in a bowl of warm water and the crystals will dissolve. Leave to cool before adding the washing-up liquid and a few drops of the essential oil of choice, if using. Transfer to the spray bottle then get to work.

Spray Pure Magic all around the greenhouse glass, inside and out, then use an old cloth and a bowl of cold water to wipe around, getting into the corners and along the ledges. Leave it for just a few minutes then hose off with cold water either from a hosepipe tap, rainwater or use a watering can. The results are astounding. I don't bother polishing the glass – just leave it to dry.

On the outside of the greenhouse check that gutters and so on are clear. Everything that has been taken outside – pots, staging and watering cans, etc. – I leave outside for a week or so and leave the greenhouse door pegged into the open position to allow lots of air to circulate. For those unsure of the term, greenhouse 'staging' is best described as a four-legged table on which to stand pots, but instead of the top being solid it is slatted so that excess water drains through to the ground below. This too gets a brush down, then I turn it upside down and allow the elements to clean up the rest and give any overwintering insects an opportunity to find somewhere else to sleep for the rest of the season.

MILK-BOTTLE UPCYCLE

Before going out to buy a selection of pots or growing tubs for the new growing season, have a think about a few upcycle ideas. Wooden boxes, plastic containers, old welly boots, an old wheelbarrow – so many items make excellent containers, and customising everyday objects is a great winter pastime. One of my favourite upcycle projects is the versatility of the everyday plastic milk bottle.

I can remember the days when the milkman visited every house to deliver their daily pint – the clink of the glass bottles as the electric milk float stopped and started on dark winter mornings. Sadly, for the majority that is no longer the case and instead milk is often bought as part of the weekly shop from the supermarket in plastic containers with a built-in handle. These plastic milk bottles do not have to be thrown into the recycling though: they have so many uses that will aid the keen gardener who has an eye for upcycling projects and can save money at the same time.

I now anxiously wait for the bottle of milk to be emptied because I have so many ideas.

The Watering Can

I have a number of four-pint plastic milk containers that have been upcycled to provide me with handy watering cans. Decorated and labelled, these are excellent and can be custom made for plant liquid feed (page 180) and just plain rainwater to keep young plants, seedlings and houseplants watered using just a fine stream of water. This is a great craft for kids too – each can decorate their own watering can and add increased interest for the budding grower.

YOU WILL NEED
2.27 litre (4 pint) used plastic milk bottle (or use a smaller
    size with a handle, the handle is the important thing)
sewing needle
permanent marker to decorate and label the bottle
naked flame (I use a gas ring) or candle

Remove the label then rinse out the bottle. Replace the cap and screw it on tightly. Take a marker pen and draw a line across the cap just below half way down from the handle side of the bottle. This will be your guide for making the water holes and making sure they are in the right place when the lid is screwed on tightly.

Remove the cap then heat the needle in the flame and make tiny holes in the smaller half of the marked cap, 8–10 holes will be sufficient – too many holes and the water will pour out too quickly in one full stream. Placing the holes above the bottom half of the cap ensures a sprinkle rather than a pour.

If your bottle fails to pour well (particularly on a small bottle), then add an air inlet hole at the top of the handle using the needle.

To decorate, set your artistic talent free and have some fun personalising the bottle, though remember to mark it as 'water' or 'plant feed', etc.

The Compost Scoop

Cut the plastic bottle in half and try to make a neat job of it so that both pieces can be used – the top half to be used as a compost scoop or planting funnel and the bottom half can be used as a simple seed pot or planter.

When cutting a plastic bottle in half I tend to make a starting hole in the centre of the bottle using a hot skewer and use this as an entry hole for my scissor blade, making it possible then to fashion a neat cut.

To use one half as a compost scoop, leave the cap in place and use the handle with the bottle neck in the upside-down position to scoop your compost from the bag to your pots or tubs. This is much better than using your hands or a trowel, and involves less spillage.

The Planting Funnel

Just as a jam funnel makes filling a narrow-necked jar easier, so does a home-made planting funnel. If, when you come to fill your small pots, just as much compost drops either side of the pot than where it should be, then this little upcycled gadget will help. This is especially useful if you sow seeds in recycled cardboard tubes because the compost can be deposited right where you want it without having to fiddle around with your hands.

Cut the bottle in half neatly then remove the cap. The open bottleneck can be slotted into the hole of the cardboard tube and fits perfectly then the compost can be tapped straight in. It can also be used for small pots too.

The Other Half!

The bottom halves of 2.27-litre (4-pint) bottles that have been used in the other milk bottle tips make perfect plant pots. I created delightful planters that are just the right size for growing cuttings from herbs, small plants and spring flowering bulbs. Spend a little more time and you have the perfect looking home-made planter gift (see page 219).

Bird Deterrent

Save the caps and tops – they can be threaded together and the strings dangled around your veggie plot later on to keep the birds off newly-sown seed beds of cabbages or peas.

STIR-FRIED LEEKS

I use leeks in soups, stews, casseroles and as a vegetable to serve with a meal. When serving leeks on their own as a green vegetable, this is my favourite way to dish them up. The colour is preserved, the flavour is amazing and – rather than an over cooked slimy sludge – the leek is shiny, beautiful, just tender and tastes delicious.

Serves 4

YOU WILL NEED
large saucepan or wok
colander (optional)

2 large leeks, trimmed and washed
2 tbsp toasted sesame oil
1 tbsp butter
small cup of frozen peas (optional)
freshly ground black pepper

Slice the washed leeks thinly and opening up the rings as you would an onion. Use the whole of the vegetable, the white and the green. If preparing ahead, place the sliced leeks in a colander and leave it outside otherwise the smell from the raw leeks will permeate your kitchen.

When ready to cook, heat the sesame oil in the large saucepan or wok over a medium heat. Sesame oil adds a lovely nutty flavour, so use this rather than your regular cooking oil. Add the butter and, just as it melts, add the leeks. Stir until all of the leeks are glossy, then add the peas (if using) and stir-fry over a high heat for 3–4 minutes, stirring regularly. Season and serve.

As I am writing this I can almost taste and smell them – delicious!

LATE WINTER

The days, thankfully, are getting longer and again the weather can be brutal and chilling but we know spring is on its way. There will be a sunny day – I promise – and the urge to get outside, get some fresh air, feel a tiny tinge of warmth from the sun on the skin, makes me impatient to get started.

Try not to be too eager. Even though garden centres and plant nurseries will have plants in stock, unless you have a heated greenhouse, don't be tempted. I have known warm temperatures in late winter and early spring, which are only followed later by snow, which can damage and kill young, tender plants.

The sun will be shining, the wind blowing and drying things out, and there will be signs of new growth around the garden. The bright sunshine and extra light encourages us to get outside to make a start.

Whatever your size of garden or growing space, you can be sure winter will have taken its toll. There will be debris, accumulations of dead leaves that have blown and collected in corners, a few weeds here and there, and tufts of grass that somehow manage to grow in abundance in the places that last year were a straight border edge.

Take some time to rake up the dry debris, pull out any overwintered weeds and redefine the lawn edges. I also like to

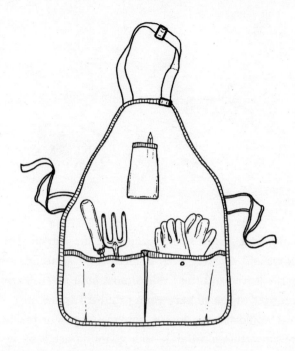

gently rake over my vegetable beds. The transformation is incredible. Walking out into the garden over the next few weeks is like walking into a newly decorated room. Tidy, clean, crisp, and just as you left it.

On those dry, cold, sunny days, use your time outside to arrange your container garden. I have a great time doing this. Varying heights and shape of container will make your garden look interesting as well as productive. I even fill some of the pots with compost partly because I am so eager to make a start, but also to prevent them blowing over in the wind. When the sun shines you have a good idea about the sunniest position for your pots, bearing in mind you will get more and more hours of sunshine as the year wakes up.

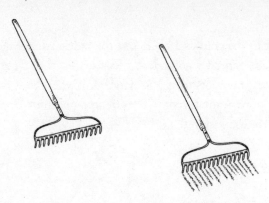

Planting

There may be signs of spring growth in the garden. The first snowdrops and aconites, even a microscopic scattering of tiny wild garlic leaves and the fresh, almost lime-green leaves and iridescent red sheen of very young rhubarb stems.

If you would like to do any new planting – or maybe you want to move things around – transplanting needs to be done while the plant is still dormant, but not when the ground is hard, frosty or waterlogged. From late winter to early spring (if the weather is being kind) I plant fruit canes, strawberries, blackcurrant bushes, redcurrants – in fact, the garden centre will be packed with lots of choice.

To know whether the conditions are right for planting and transplanting, I consider whether the conditions feel right for me. If I can walk onto my garden without my boots becoming blathered in mud, I am feeling comfortable in a couple of jumpers and a fleece, I don't need a hat and I'm enjoying my time outside, then I consider that the conditions are probably perfect.

If, on the other hand, my time outside is a quick dash when the wind is blowing and burning my face and hands, turning my back to the cold as I clean out the chickens, dig up a leek or two and harvest a colander of kale leaves, then as a plant I would want my roots to stay underground where they can keep warm. I don't want to come outside and certainly don't want to move house just yet!

Pruning

Late winter is also a good time to tidy up shrubs, trees and bushes if they are looking misshapen or overgrown. As a general rule (for both the sake of the plant or tree and for any over-wintering insects hidden in the nooks and crannies), and if in any doubt, a gentle prune is better than cutting very hard back. Don't do any cutting if there is frost or snow on the ground.

If there are bushes, shrubs or small trees in the garden and you would like to reduce their size or tidy up their shape but are not sure what to do, start off with a gentle snip here and there.

Any overwintering small animals and insects are unlikely to be disturbed from their slumbers and then you can always cut back some more if necessary when growth starts and all insects are awake and on the move.

When you take a close look, it is not unusual to see clusters of ladybirds – maybe ten or more – huddled together in the most unlikely places. I have seen them, usually positioned in a south-facing group under windowsills, under branches and hidden away at the back of the BBQ.

Little wooden ladybird houses are a great gift idea for the keen gardener, however ladybirds and other insects can also find a suitable home themselves – we just have to be mindful of our actions in the garden to make sure we give them the protection they need. Ladybirds and many other insects help the organic gardener immensely, munching their way through greenfly, whitefly and aphids. It is important that we nurture them.

If you want to prune but are not sure what to do, start with any dead and dry branches. After removing them, seek out the unruly branch or stem that may be spoiling the compact or neat shape of the plant and, once you have decided, then look closely for a bud. It is just above this bud that you need to make your cut.

Cut just above an outward facing bud that will encourage new growth outwards away from the centre of the shrub or bush. Don't cut above an inwards facing bud as the new growth will grow into the centre of the shrub, causing it to become crowded with branches criss-crossing, rubbing against each other and encouraging damage and disease. The shape will not improve and next year you could find yourself back to square one and wondering why your prune didn't seem to help at all.

If you have heard the Yorkshire saying 'If in doubt – do nowt!', I certainly apply that rule to pruning.

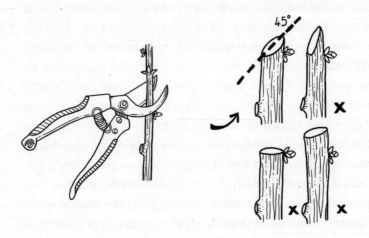

HOUSEPLANT HEALTH-CHECK

Houseplants are enjoying a comeback. They were very popular in the 1970s and I remember being very much a part of the trend! Every home, office, pub, library and even our doctor's surgery seemed to be showing off their ever-growing (in size and popularity) cheese plant, spider plant and yucca!

We used to make our own plant hangers from string for the huge spiders with their cascading offspring, cheese plants were positioned on upstairs landings and encouraged to throw their huge dinner plate-sized leaves through the spindles of staircases and a prize yucca occupied a corner spot next to many a TV.

Fifty years on, it seems we have once more fallen in love with the houseplant. I read in *Gardeners' World* magazine that in recent years houseplant sales have increased by 50 per cent! People are wanting to grow more both inside and outside, and not just for food but for pleasure too. I have to admit I went through a stage of having a few silk replicas over the years but now find myself discarding these dust-collectors and bringing more real plants into the home. There is something very pleasing and uplifting about a leafy collection of plants in a room, kitchen or conservatory – and they love bathrooms!

I have created a little 'working-from-home' garden made up of a selection of small, easy-to-grow houseplants including succulents, a tiny glass vase of seasonal flowers from the garden which I change regularly, home-made hanging planters and upcycled and decorated plastic planting pots. The window space is packed with colour, down from the wooden frame above to the windowsill below. I cannot tell you how much pleasure it gives me when I am writing and pausing for thought – this little 'window' of natural colour and perfume is so much more pleasing to the eye than the twenty-year-old photo of me sitting on a park bench in Dublin which my working-from-home garden replaced!

If you have houseplants, it is important to remember they are living things, not inert ornaments to dust around once a week. A winter spent indoors can be a tough time for them. The central heating dries up the atmosphere and, with reduced light, they can look (and may also feel) out of sorts.

A regular fine spray mist with rainwater is extremely beneficial to houseplants even though they don't need to be watered much during the winter. When they do display a covering of dust, a wipe with moistened kitchen paper for large-leafed plants or a spray under the shower will give any indoor plant a refreshing pick-me-up.

Houseplants are often ignored as they become part of the furniture and only when they show signs of stress do we notice something may be wrong. You may see a layer of fluffy mould growing on the surface of the compost, which is usually a sign that the plant has been overwatered. Overwatering plants in the winter when they are dormant will mean the moisture sits in the pot, soaking and water logging the roots, growing fungus and – at worst – rotting the plant. Think of yourself asleep in bed, not needing food or water yet it is being poured all over you – yuck. When I have been guilty of overwatering and water logging a plant (when I take the pot from its planter to see it standing in an inch or two of water) I take it outside, stand it on a rack so that any excess water can freely drain out, fluff up the top layer of soil with a fork to let the air in and leave it in the fresh air and sunshine for a day or two. If the weather is cold or frost is in the air, then this needs to be done inside on the sink drainer or in a greenhouse. Very often the plant looks rejuvenated and lush again once excess moisture is removed.

Houseplant Feed

Commercial organic houseplant feeds can be expensive, so I did some reading, got my thinking cap on and came up with this little home-made recipe. I have been using it for some time now and my plants seem to like it. Starting in late winter or early spring – or when there are signs of new growth – I give them one liquid feed in a month, I find this is sufficient to be given when the plants are growing. I use it for all of my houseplants and none of them have been any the worse for it.

I was unsure about whether to feed my two Christmas cactus plants, so I tried a simple experiment. I gave just one the feed, leaving the other with just water, and although I was 'willing' my fed plant on, talking to it every day, it did appear more lush, well-nourished and healthier than its neighbour.

I have a huge jade plant that was given to me as a small 7.5cm (3 inch) pot plant many years ago. It now stands on the ground in the conservatory, is about 1.2 metres (4 feet) tall and 91cm (3 feet) wide and is a beauty. I water it very little in the winter and, even though I read that my gorgeous jade plant doesn't need a feed, I decided to give it a 'shot' once every two weeks as well as a regular weekly watering routine. To my delight, and for the first time I can remember, by late spring it was covered in tiny white flowers and looked so beautiful – I will continue with my feed!

The Epsom salt contains magnesium and sulphur which is loved by plants. The magnesium is good for foliage, helping plants to retain their green colour, and it enhances flower blooming. The sulphur helps them to absorb valuable nutrients. The bicarbonate of soda is a good fungal and mildew deterrent, and the coffee, which contains nitrogen, is a great pick-me-up for plants as it is a major component of chlorophyll, the compound by which plants use sunlight energy to produce sugars from water and carbon dioxide (you may have heard of photosynthesis).

YOU WILL NEED
6g (¼oz) Epsom salt
2g bicarbonate of soda
small jug
60ml (2fl oz) hot strong black coffee – use real not instant
    (no milk or sugar)
recycled 1-litre (34fl oz) plastic bottle
rainwater (or tap water), to top up

Weigh the Epsom salt and bicarbonate of soda in a small jug then add the hot black coffee and stir until the salts have dissolved. Pour this into the recycled plastic bottle then top up to 1 litre (34fl oz) with rainwater. I pour 1 tablespoon of this clear amber liquid into the soil around my very small house plants and give my large floor-standing jade plant 4 tablespoons.

Coffee Feed

An even quicker and simpler dilute nitrogen feed for house-plants and veggies can be made from just 150g (5½oz) coffee grounds topped up to 1 litre (34fl oz) with rainwater, stirred well, then left to settle overnight so that the solids drop to the bottom. Pour the liquid into an old plastic squirty bottle (the leftover grounds can be tossed into the compost) and spray your plants once a month. I squirt the liquid feed at the base of plants outside and directly into the pot for houseplants – about 1 tablespoon each squirt.

‖‖‖

TIP: I always add coffee grounds and tea leaves to the compost pile. I prefer to do this rather than add them direct to the soil around plants. I know some gardeners scatter grounds around plants, but I tried this one year and found that the coffee grounds turned mouldy on the surface and the plants didn't seem to benefit at all. I prefer them to decompose along with everything else in the compost bin (see Create Compost on page 25).

‖‖‖

SEASONAL SPECIAL – PLANTING SWEET PEAS

I usually save the fun job of planting up sweet peas for Valentine's Day. Sweet peas sown on Valentine's Day should give you your first bunch of cut flowers exactly four months later, on 14th June, and they will continue flowering relentlessly until the end of September if you look after them. They are inexpensive too. Once you have bought your first packet of seeds, you can be self-sufficient for years to come if you save your own seeds at the start of autumn (see page 189).

If you have been saving up cardboard tubes, now is the time to put your home-made upcycled gadgets to use: I sow sweet peas and garden peas in tubes because they grow a long tap root that doesn't then need to be disturbed when transplanting and use my funnel and compost scoop (see page 274) and plant two seeds per tube.

Holding the funnel by the handle, scoop up the compost then position it over the tube and tap gently until the compost fills 2.5–5cm (1–2 inches) of the tube. Now compact this first layer of compost so that it doesn't fall out when picked up – a wooden stick pushed down on the compost in the tube will do this perfectly. Fill the rest of the tube right to the top using the funnel.

There are strong shallow cardboard boxes that contain small oranges – I always buy two or three at Christmas time, put them to one side and bring them out now as they make a perfect sturdy tray for holding around 12 or so filled cardboard tubes side by side in an upright position. Even after watering, the cardboard will remain robust to support the tubes and growing peas - yet can be pulled apart easily and added to the compost as a dry layer once the sweet peas have gone into the ground. Alternatively, of course, sweet peas can be sown two per 7.5cm (3 inch) pot to be planted out later. The box of cardboard tubes can be placed in an unheated greenhouse or on the windowsill in a cold yet frost free room.

Sweet peas are hardy little plants, and the first shoots will appear about two weeks after sowing. What starts off as a tiny arrow poking through the soil will readily develop into a little plant bearing two sets of leaves. When you see the stem continue to grow and ready to grow another set of leaves, pinch out this latest shoot, back to the second pair of leaves. This encourages the plant to grow outwards rather than upwards. The little plant will then change direction and start to throw out side shoots, resulting in a compact bushy plant that will produce more flowers than one single stem.

I have had followers send me screenshots of their prize sweet-pea plants that have unfortunately grown leggy. The plants have been kept too warm and not given sufficient light, and the result is a very long stem with the tiniest of pale coloured leaves. Any healthy seedling should be compact with strong healthy robust looking dark leaves.

As your sweet peas start to grow and flourish, you will notice areas of the cardboard tube begin to grow spots of mould. This is perfectly normal and these are the first signs of decomposition. Don't be alarmed, certainly don't throw them away and don't overwater the plants either. By the time the sweet peas are ready to go outside, the cardboard will have roots growing through it as it has softened. Once the cardboard tube is very soft and decomposing, with maybe a few spots of mould here and there, with roots coming out of the bottom and even pushing their way out of the sides, then they are ready to go outside – usually by late spring (May in the UK).

The benefit of planting sweet peas in cardboard tubes is that, apart from not using a plastic pot, the whole lot can go into the ground. The cardboard will finish decomposing completely and the roots will spread themselves readily having not been disturbed during the transplanting.

Sweet peas need a few things in order to flourish: they need to not be competing with weeds, so make sure the chosen area is clear, they need to be kept well-watered, they need to be cut regularly and not allowed to form seed pods, and they need to be able to climb. When you first take your plants outside as little bushes about 20cm (8 inches) tall, plant them about 15–20cm (6–8 inches) apart, around a pyramid-type construction made from windfall branches, tree prunings or canes. Weave jute twine (compostable string) between the canes to offer each plant a handle to grab onto on its race to the top.

Take a look at your seed packet (always hang onto them to refer to later) to find out how tall your sweet peas will grow and ensure your frame is at least that size, otherwise your plants will reach the top then flop over. As your not-so-little plants soon get hold of their climbing frame, they'll be off. You will see the thin tendrils reaching out and then grabbing hold of the first piece of string or wire, wrapping itself then so tight so that it can climb ever higher.

Just as an aside, I now have a permanent growing frame because the tree prunings I used two years ago took root themselves! One thing I have learnt about gardening and growing is that plants, seeds, cuttings – in fact anything – really *wants* to grow. It is clear that plants will grow in spite of me and not because of me.

A GOOD YEAR:
ROUND-UP

The clock doesn't stop as one year comes to a close, because already it is the time to look forward to the next one – another cycle of seasons. The frustrations that the year presented, to know or maybe not quite know what to do differently next time, the successes, the fun, the exercise, the outdoors, the learning – all of it is good for us.

It may be cold and dark outside but it's perfect thinking time inside: short winter days and long dark evenings are the perfect time to put your feet up and make a few notes. Your garden plans for next year may well start in early winter (see page 298) so it is worth making notes and writing down a few lines about problems you encountered, plus the successes. I find a few photos on my phone taken at the time are a great source of information and a reminder too of how wonderful the spring and summer were.

When sitting down to consider your next growing year, ponder, stare at the ceiling and ask yourself the following questions:

- What went well this year?
- What did you learn this year?
- For those new to growing – how big do you want to the growing space to be and how much space have you got?
- For experienced growers – have you plans to extend your vegetable plot or grow more next year?

I find that, not intentionally, my head begins buzzing with these questions. I sit with my A4 diary, scribble down a few notes and glance back at the seasons' entries of ups and downs. Here are a few examples of the type of notes I might make:

Tomatoes, potatoes and beetroot did very well this year, so much so I have stocks in the garage and many jars of fresh tomato sauce on the shelf.

I learned that it is probably necessary to hand-pollinate my Luffa plants – I left it too late this year and only pollinated two but the next growing season I will know exactly what to look for.

I learned this year that growing basil from seed is no longer necessary – I can grow it quicker and more cheaply, and with less work, if I take cuttings from a supermarket pot.

My celeriac roots were the best I have every grown I will hope for even bigger bulbs next year and the secret is not to ever let them dry out.

I plan to grow more Charlotte potatoes because they are delicious, had no holes or blemishes and stored so well and kept me going well into early winter.

Remember not to plant a trailing bush tomato plant in a low growing position. It spreads all over the ground and the tomatoes end up getting squashed – plant in a hanging basket!

I love working outside, getting my hands into the earth and not worrying about my nails, hair, or clothes, but instead listening to the birds, and getting up close and personal to watch insects doing their thing while they help to keep us fed and nourished. I find it wondrous how every living thing has its own role and job to do in enabling our natural world to carry on functioning.

Food is fundamental to life and the joy of seeing a tiny seed develop into a huge crop which then goes on to produce its own seeds so that the cycle of life can continue seems so simple and obvious, yet is an absolute wonder of nature. I mean, we only have to consider the courgette – one small seed can produce up to 50 fruits! This cycle applies to every species.

Times are changing and affordable food is becoming scarce for a variety of reasons. I consider it is as important now as it ever has been that we allow nature to take the lead and help teach us how to behave. We don't need to interfere that much – plants actually want to grow, insects want to pollinate, and they are our friends. Once we understand that insects and bugs are beneficial to the modern gardener, they are not to be considered an inconvenience to us and something that has to be sprayed, swatted and destroyed. They have as much right to be here as we have, and they have a purpose – we just need to work alongside them and steer our growing and planting habits accordingly.

Up until now, I believe the human race has confidently believed it can control and manipulate the planet and its natural resources. There are so many practices we have adopted, such as overuse of chemical fertilisers, dependence on the need for spraying to kill insects and disease, and our indiscriminate use of plastics has resulted in the pollution of our waters and oceans – to name just a few – but our planet has hit back. Extreme weather events and global warming warn us about the dangers if we continue with our actions.

In a bid to minimise my own personal impact on the planet, I have adopted a practice of thinking about what I actually *need* rather than what I think I *want* – the two are very different. Applying this principle just to food (never mind clothing and other consumer 'must haves') has helped me to reduce the amount of food I buy. Food waste is obscene and unnecessary. I believe that once we understand where things come from – the long time it takes for it to grow and the abundance that Mother Nature actually provides – we cannot and should not waste it. This all becomes apparent when we begin to grow our own food; there is a greater understanding about seasonality, availability, taste and nutrition. Involving children and capturing their interest is the most exciting way forward of all – they are the future.

Thankfully, there is now a heightened awareness about the need to reduce food waste and respect the food that is produced. There are actions taking place by us the consumers, and supermarkets are now doing more to help us to buy sensibly, relaxing some expiry dates on food items and celebrating 'wonky' produce. These pledges, and more of a willingness to change long-held habits, combined with a growing respect for our gorgeous planet will, in time be adopted by enough people so that the wasteful way that we are living and consuming will become a thing of the past.

I sincerely hope there will be less of a reliance on imported foods when they can be easily be grown locally, and even by us at home. We can waste less as we learn and get into the habit of buying seasonal food and we will then go on to use every morsel. Not only are we helping to save the planet, we are saving money too.

Am I sad and in despair about the state of our planet? Am I worried and concerned for our children? Do I think it is all a lost cause? My final thought to you, my dear readers, is that I am inspired and energised. Not a day goes by that a social media follower doesn't message me, sending me screenshots of a germinated seed, of them encouraging their children to start a small garden, or creating a mini balcony hothouse out of recycled items. I am delighted and encouraged by the changes being made by my family, friends and followers and that is just among my one small circle of people.

You can multiply this by the number of changes being made by other individuals, by governments, by large organisations, but most importantly it is those everyday small changes by individuals – the likes of you and me – that matter. Once people care enough and begin to engage with our world, become interested and aware of how it is, how things have changed and what now needs to happen – only then will the people in power be pressured to take action. I can only speak for myself here, but there is no doubt that living a greener life is addictive in a 'feel good' kind of way, and makes me feel a whole lot better about myself and the planet and offers some comfort for what the world will be like for generations to come.

As I sit here in my garden with a cuppa in the sunshine, I am listening to the birds and the bees and thoroughly enjoying the peace, the warmth from the sun and admiring my own little corner of paradise. Then, what I do see as I look up at the birds: not a clear cloudless sky but a huge raincloud overhead. Am I disappointed that I cannot enjoy the sunshine today for not much longer? In the past I would have grumbled, 'Oh no – not rain again – just when I want to sit here with my drink!' 'Hang on a minute', I now say to myself, 'this isn't just about you.' The veggies need a drink, the flowers and birds too. I see a honeybee seemingly crash-land and take a seat beside me on a leaf edge and then pause to take a breather. She is probably totally exhausted following a journey which could well have been in the region of five miles. She is in much need of a drink! The first raindrops fall and there it is – she sips at a droplet just collected in the hollow of a leaf. Her needs just now are much greater than mine.

This planet isn't just about what I need – we all have needs. We must live and let live. My life, the lives of everyone else and the lives and wellbeing of every other living thing that make up our living planet means that we are all part of a very complex mix of checks and balances that are working flexibly in order that things can and are able to run along smoothly.

Our planet is a true wonder and something I like to think of as an enormous jigsaw. This giant of a puzzle is bigger than we can imagine, it has many pieces, and each piece represents one of nature's own living things – me included. Some pieces may be very large, others very small, but each one is important and has its own role to play. In order to understand nature and our planet I think we need to see it as a complex yet living thing – the whole picture needs to be appreciated. Each of the pieces has a place and purpose. Each jigsaw piece slots together perfectly and once each one clicks into place we understand and see this wonderful colourful living picture that nature surely is.

I can think of a number of jigsaw pieces that I helped to fit together; I saw for myself how perfect it was that all of the pieces joined up. I refer to my sacrificial nasturtiums planted among my fruit bushes. They attracted the butterflies that went on to feed the resultant caterpillars, blackfly and aphids. The well-fed insects went on to feed the ladybirds, frogs, toads and birds. My blackcurrant bushes, very grateful to the nasturtiums, then needed no sprays or protection from insect infestation themselves and went on fruit abundantly to then be harvested and used to feed me. My corner of the jigsaw slotted together very well indeed.

Consider your own garden, allotment, balcony or even sunny windowsill to be your own version of this huge planet-jigsaw and watch and learn how satisfying it is when you have helped a number of moving parts to readily click into place.

We know how to do the right thing . . . let's do it!

QUICK REFERENCE CROP GUIDE

Here is my rough guide which I hope will help you to navigate your own growing space and allow you to think about what could go where and when various veggies will be ready to harvest. This list is by no means exhaustive but these are the crops I grow year on year because they are easy, resilient and many that are not eaten immediately will store, preserve or freeze beautifully. Read the section on companion planting on page 114 to further help plan your veggies and their place in your growing space.

	SPRING	SUMMER	AUTUMN	WINTER
Courgettes	Sow in pots indoors or under glass	Plant out into beds or below sweetcorn then start to harvest	Continue harvesting	
Beetroot	Sow direct into the soil then pinch out	Harvest	Store in sand	
Broad beans	Sow direct and a few spares into pots	Harvest and freeze for winter use	Freezer store	

Carrots	Sow direct into the soil	Harvest, repeat sowings as necessary	Harvest autumn varieties	
Cauliflower	Sow under glass then prick out and plant out	Harvest, blanch and freeze	Freezer store	
Celeriac	Sow, prick out and plant out	Growing	Harvest	
Courgettes	Sow in pots	Plant into beds or below sweetcorn then start to harvest	Harvest	
Cucumbers	Start seeds in propa-gator or under glass then pot on	Grow under glass, harvest midsummer and make pickle	Pickled store	
French beans	Sow in pots and plant out or sow direct into the soil late spring	Harvest, blanch and freeze	Harvest dried pods for seed or kitchen use	Freezer and dried store
Kale	Sow indoors or under glass and plant out	Growing	Harvest	
Leeks	Sow direct into the soil	Plant out to final growing space	Harvest	

Onions and garlic	Growing	Harvest and store for autumn and winter use	Plant	Growing
Parsnips (Y1)	Sow direct into the soil then pinch out	Growing	Harvest	
Parsnips (Y2)	Transplant previous year's roots	Flowering	Collect seeds	Store seeds
Peas	Sow late spring under nets, then give climbing twigs	Harvest, blanch and freeze	Freezer store	
Peppers and chillies	Start seeds in propagator or under glass then pot on	Grow under glass and outdoors. Harvest	Harvest, freeze and make chilli sauce	Freezer store
Potatoes	Plant out	Harvest then cure to store	Stored in paper sacks	Chit seed potatoes
Raspberries (autumn)	Grow in same bed each year	Flowering	Harvest and freeze	Cut down to ground level after last fruits, apply compost or leaf mould
Raspberries (summer)	Grow in same bed each year	Harvest, freeze or preserve for winter use	Cut back and secure new growth onto wires	Apply compost or leaf mould

Rhubarb	Harvest	Harvest until midsummer	Split crown if necessary	Apply compost
Runner beans	Sow in pots and plant out or sow direct into the ground late spring	Harvest and make pickle	Collect seeds from dried pods	Save for seed or kitchen use
Salads	Sow salad seeds under glass or indoors every 3 weeks	Harvest and re-sow	Harvest and re-sow	
Savoy cabbage	Sow indoors or under glass and plant out	Harvest		
Spinach	Sow direct into the ground then pinch out	Growing	Harvest	
Spring cabbage	Harvest	Sow outdoors in seed bed	Plant out to final spacing	Growing
Sprouts	Sow indoors and plant out or plant into the soil late spring	Growing	Stake tall plants	Harvest
Strawberries	Protect from birds with nets	Harvest and make freezer jam	Cut back or root new plants	Freezer jam store
Swede	Sow and pinch out	Growing	Harvest	Harvest

Sweetcorn	Sow under glass and pot on until garden space is available	Plant after onions	Harvest	
Tomatoes	Start seeds in propagator or under glass then pot on	Grow under glass or outdoors	Harvest, make passata	Freezer store of passata

KEEPS FOR UP TO . . .
STORING VEGGIES AND FRUIT

Wrap veggies in a dampened cloth and keep in the salad compartment in the fridge (see page 59). Re-dampen once a week – I do this on Saturdays.

ITEM	KEEPS FOR UP TO . . .
Carrot	6 months
Kale	2 weeks
Broccoli	2 weeks
Parsnip	3 months
Celery	6 weeks
Swede, whole	5 weeks
Swede, half	2 weeks
Courgette	6 weeks
Rhubarb	3 weeks
Herbs	3 weeks
Peppers	2 weeks
Spinach	4 weeks
Cucumber	4 weeks

Soft berries washed in a citric acid bath (see pages 61-2).

ITEM	KEEPS FOR UP TO . . .
Strawberries	2 weeks
Raspberries	2 weeks
Blueberries	3 weeks

Store the following in a sealed jar of water (see page 60).

ITEM	KEEPS FOR UP TO . . .
Lemon	15 weeks
Lime	4–6 weeks (then colour pales)
Chives	1 week
Half Lemon	2 weeks
Half Apple	2 weeks
Half Onion	1 week

Other items.

ITEM	KEEPS FOR UP TO . . .
Mushrooms, stored in a dry cloth	2 weeks
Salad leaves, washed, in a sealed plastic box	2 weeks
Banana kept in a sealed plastic box in the fridge	3 weeks

Acknowledgements

This book has been around sixty years in the writing, I say tongue in cheek! Though, on a serious note, it wasn't until I began writing down my gardening and growing experiences – some elements going back to growing alongside my grandad as a young child – that I appreciated at least two things I hadn't given much thought to before: One, the magnificence of the human brain's long term data storage facility and two, the surprise at how much information I had gathered over the years, packed into my memory that I have been able to retrieve.

I sat myself down – a 6am start many mornings for a whole year and documented my gardening and growing knowledge through the seasons. It has been fun to draw on experiences both old and new along with my usual stories of 'ups and downs' along the way. So – here we are – *The Green Gardening Handbook*! I haven't been able to do this all on my own, we all need help and support and so I would like to take this opportunity to give thanks.

Firstly, my publisher Pan Macmillan who signed me up once again and especially the fabulous team at One Boat. In particular I want to give enormous thanks to Hockley for her professional attitude and attention to the very smallest detail. This has been our third book together and her help and guidance is uplifting and encouraging and a tremendous help in enabling me to enjoy writing.

My agents and friends at Yellow Poppy Media who continue to manage my diary commitments and workload and are available day and night with support, help and advice.

My followers, many of whom have been with me a long time and have been inspired by my posts to grow their own food too – and great results I might add! A thank you too for the early reviewers and their encouraging feedback of this book and I hope it inspires others in the same way.

My family and friends who acknowledge that my 'Greenness' is here to stay. I thank them for their patience when I may not seem to have spare time because I have my head, thoughts and motivation into some new green recipe or tip or money saving hack. However, I notice now that even they too are beginning to embrace a more responsible way of living – whether it be household cleaning recipes from *Clean and Green*, everyday lifestyle changes from *Green Living Made Easy*, and now hopefully a move towards growing some of their own food from *Green Gardening*.

Not forgetting Dave, who is my compost connoisseur and shares my enthusiasm for this wonderful natural gorgeousness. Many a conversation has been had on the subject of high temperatures – not of the weather, but of the maximum reading on the compost thermometer.

Last but by no means least – Tim (often referred to as 'Him Indoors') though in truth he spends the majority of his time outdoors. Without him being there every single day I doubt I could do what I do. He is very good at helping me to structure my work, remind me of the important things in life, do the heavy jobs around the garden, yet turn up with a cup of tea at just the right time. The garden is a good place for us both – our happy place, I call it. We each have our jobs and areas of expertise and I am delighted he is finally beginning to warm to nasturtiums!

I hope you enjoy this book and that you find yourself dipping in and out throughout the year, taking ideas and inspiration from some of my experiences. I have thoroughly enjoyed writing it and will continue to grow my own food in a green and sustainable way – I hope you do too!

Author Biography

Nancy Birtwhistle is a *Sunday Times* bestselling author, lifelong gardener and Hull-born baker who won the fifth series of *The Great British Bake Off* in 2014. Motivated by protecting the planet for her ten grandchildren, Nancy decided to change how she used plastic, single use products and chemicals in her home. Sharing her tips online, she amassed an engaged international following of devoted fans interested not only in her delicious recipes, but also her innovative ideas and time-saving swaps that rethink everyday house and garden tasks to make as little an impact on the environment as possible. Nancy worked as a GP practice manager in the NHS for thirty-six years until she retired in 2007. She lives in Lincolnshire with her husband, dogs and rescue hens.

Connect with Nancy on Instagram: @nancy.birtwhistle, on Twitter: @nancybbakes, on Tiktok: @nancy_birtwhistle or through her website: nancybirtwhistle.co.uk

Portrait by Mel Four.

INDEX

seeds and sowing 40, 45, 247, 263
split 10, 142
storing 62
tomato passata 171–4
tomato skins 173
tools 16–19, 20, 217, 268
tulips 92
turnips 106–7, 116, 118

V

vanilla pods 79
vegetables: blanching 151–2, 153
cooking frozen 153
quick reference guide 298–302
storing 57–60, 151–2, 303

vegetable powder 171
waste nothing stock 170–1
see also individual types of vegetable

W

watering 23, 43, 139, 285
watering can, milk-bottle 273–4
weeds and weeding 34, 93–4, 101–2, 278
wild garlic 70, 74–6
wild garlic seasoning 75–6
wildlife 21
winter 229–30, 237–90
winter wash 247–50
worms 32–3

Notes